GETTING STARTED IN BALLET

Students from the School of Madison Ballet, Madison, Wisconsin. © 2015
Maureen Janson

SECOND EDITION

GETTING STARTED
IN BALLET

A Parent's Guide to Dance Education

ANNA PASKEVSKA

REVISED BY MAUREEN JANSON

OXFORD
UNIVERSITY PRESS

OXFORD
UNIVERSITY PRESS

Oxford University Press is a department of the University of Oxford. It furthers
the University's objective of excellence in research, scholarship, and education
by publishing worldwide. Oxford is a registered trademark of Oxford University
Press in the UK and certain other countries.

Published in the United States of America by Oxford University Press
198 Madison Avenue, New York, NY 10016, United States of America.

© Oxford University Press 2016

First Edition published in 1997
Second Edition published in 2016

Library of Congress Cataloging-in-Publication Data
Paskevska, Anna.
Getting started in ballet : a parent's guide to dance education / Anna Paskevska with Maureen
Janson. — Second edition.
pages cm
Summary: "From selecting a teacher in the early stages, to supporting a child through his
or her choice to dance professionally, Getting Started in Ballet, A Parent's Guide to Dance
Education leads parents of prospective dancers through a full range of considerations,
encouraging careful thinking and informed decision-making when embarking on dance
training"— Provided by publisher.
Includes bibliographical references and index.
ISBN 978-0-19-022619-0 (paperback) — ISBN 978-0-19-022618-3 (hardcover)
1. Ballet—Study and teaching.   2. Dance schools.   I. Janson, Maureen.   II. Title.
GV1788.5.P377 2016
792.8'071—dc23

To Boris, Tamela and Tatiana, Theo,
Linda and little Theo and Brianna, and to Nadezhda

For Claude, Mom, and Dad

CONTENTS

FOREWORD

Becoming a dancer, a lifetime quest, involves more than talent, desire, and discipline. These are the stones for the building of a house. They remain only that unless there is a structure, and that cannot be accomplished without a design. *Getting Started in Ballet* is a book intended to assist in the design of a dancer's life. Like a knowledgeable architect, Ms. Paskevska speaks to us about the issues and concerns in the creation of that course, so that dancers, or anyone involved with the guidance of a dancer, can make informed decisions each step of the way.

Getting Started in Ballet is an invaluable source book. Using her knowledge and inspirations based on a life in dance, professionally and personally, Ms. Paskevska guides us developmentally through matters crucial to a dancer's full realization. She does this with information that is backed up by academic research and personal anecdotes.

A true cornerstone toward a celestial architecture, I found *Getting Started in Ballet* informative and enjoyable.

Violette Verdy

PREFACE

Much has changed since this book was first published and it is my great honor to help bring forth this second edition. Although the foundation of ballet technique training has remained virtually unaltered for centuries, over the past 20 years (since the first issue of this book) our technologically influenced world has expanded the way we give and receive information. The overall approach to training in ballet has been refreshed within these pages to include supplemental dance styles and conditioning methods that are now commonplace in dance training. Secondary education and career opportunities in dance have grown since the 1990s, also something presented here. The infusion of these ideas and more shed new, exciting light on *Getting Started in Ballet*. At the heart of this second volume, which blends Anna Paskevska's original writing and philosophy with a few upgrades and expansions, is the hope that the parents of a novice, promising, or preprofessional dancer enter into the art form along with their child, and do so with a solid understanding of and appreciation for dance, and ballet in particular. I first met Ms. Paskevska as a student ballet major in her classes within the dance department at Indiana University. To say that her teaching, wisdom, kindness, dedication, and heart inspired me is an understatement. She was a life-changing force for me. I had the good fortune to receive her guidance through that formative time of my career, and over the following years I grew to credit her as a mentor and to look to her for continued learning in dance and in life. Having assisted Ms. Paskevska with several writing endeavors, I was most pleased when she originally decided to compile this book—to share with prospective dance parents insights that had felt so important and influential to me, many that I had adopted as a young teacher. This edition is still peppered with Ms. Paskevska's wonderful quirky anecdotes and sage advice, while addressing our contemporary world in an inviting and thorough way. With a good support network (starting with you, the parent) and a bit of knowledge going in, anyone can be given the chance to experience dance, discover its magic, and perhaps pursue it for life. It has been an honor and pleasure to revisit and work with Ms. Paskevska's language, theories, and thoughts, and to help guide them into a new context while staying true to the long-lasting traditions of the beautiful art form of ballet.

Maureen Janson

ACKNOWLEDGMENTS

Special thanks to Claude Heintz, Selene Carter, W. Earle Smith, Alyssa Gunsolus, the School of Madison Ballet, Emily Stein, Sibyl Spalinger, Lisa Thurrell, Maribeth Kisner-Griffin, Norman Hirschy, Peg and Gene Janson, and to all who have helped in numerous ways, especially those who patiently listened as I discussed the many aspects and challenges of assembling this revised edition.

In loving memory of Anna Paskevska

Students from the School of Madison Ballet, Madison, Wisconsin. © 2015
Maureen Janson

INTRODUCTION

You want to take your child to a dance class: where do you go? How do you know that the school presented on a website will be suitable? Which type of classes will be most beneficial? Because dancers train from an early age, the parents' choice of a first teacher, and the advice and support through the years of training, are central to their development. Even if neither the child nor the parents envision dance as a profession but simply look for a meaningful extracurricular activity, the choices are best guided by some knowledge of the field.

The dance profession is both more exciting and more demanding than anyone standing on the outside can apprehend. It is exciting not only because of the gala occasions, but in subtle and personal ways—feeling the total stretch of a leg, experiencing the headiness of multiple turns, arriving at a level of technique when the motion takes over and step follows step without conscious effort or mental deliberation. And it is demanding because dance is all-encompassing.

Children may give up a social life to attend classes and rehearsals and put up with tired muscles. A professional will persevere knowing that there may be few material rewards, little security, and possible physical discomfort. Proper training and awareness of the obstacles can ease the dancer's experience.

In these pages teachers will learn to understand the role of the dance parent, and parents will find questions answered, concerns addressed, and an overview of the unique world of dance.

GETTING STARTED IN BALLET

In creative movement, students learn how to express their ideas and imaginings, while improving balance and coordination. Students from the School of Madison Ballet, Madison, Wisconsin. © 2015 Maureen Janson

WHY DANCE?

FOR HUMAN BEINGS, DANCING IS as natural as breathing. We have forgotten how our ancestors danced or why they danced, but children remember. My granddaughter at six months would begin rocking as soon as she heard music. A conversation with prospective students' parents frequently begins: "Jenny is always dancing, around the kitchen, in the living room . . ." How old is Jenny? Typically she is about two or three.

Why do we dance? There is no single answer to cover all reasons. In the past, humankind danced in worship and celebration. In the Western tradition, social dance has occupied a very special place: we dance for the pleasure it gives us. The tradition of classical ballet has its roots in the social dances at the courts of the European kings. We dance to entertain others, or we dance to share our feelings or the feelings of the role we portray. At a more pedestrian level, we dance because it is a good exercise. We learn to dance to promote good posture, to burn off calories, to become more graceful. All of the above reasons have one factor in common—through the act of dance we experience a sense of communality. We share, express, or communicate our sense of well-being through motion.

When modern dance icon Isadora Duncan was asked at what age she started dancing, she replied, "In the womb." Acclaimed choreographer Martha Graham said that she did not choose to dance; dance chose her. Indeed, dance is seldom a conscious decision; when the time comes to make a commitment to serious training, the dance is in the blood of those who have been chosen. To stop dancing seems as inconceivable as to stop breathing.

Although not everyone is born to be a professional dancer, dance training benefits all. It establishes an awareness of the body, and an appreciation for what the body can do. It also aids in the physical and mental development of the child.

A study conducted by William Greenough at the University of Illinois has linked the development of synaptic connections in the brain to simple physical tasks repeated many times. "When you exercise vigorously and regularly, you are not only changing your muscles . . . you are changing your brain . . . Improving the brain's ability to respond efficiently to one form of exercise also prepares it to better handle other types of physical activities" (*Chicago Tribune,* 1991). Greenough suggests that exercise is good because it enlarges the brain's capacity to respond to a variety of stimuli: "When the environment demands extensive repetition of a small set of simple, well practiced movements, the vascular support is altered to handle the increased metabolic load and is associated with higher levels of neural activity." In other words, repetition of a movement practice such as the one that ballet training provides aids the circulatory system and in turn, the central nervous system and the brain.

The fields of science and medicine have turned to dance in conducting studies to discover its potential to unlock the mysteries of Alzheimer's disease. A 2003 study published in the *New England Journal of Medicine* compared various activities for their potential to stave off dementia. Dance emerged as the activity most likely to keep it at bay. Promising results have also been found through recent studies using dance and movement as therapy for people with Parkinson's disease.

Dance is also of great benefit in the social sphere. Unlike playing video games on a personal electronic device, children participating in a dance class become aware of spatial relationships and learn how to work in harmony with each other. In this noncompetitive environment they learn about cooperation and support of each other's efforts. In creative movement or preballet classes, they also learn how to express their ideas and imaginings, thereby improving their communication skills.

In a 2015 public television special called *P.S. Dance!*, Catherine Gallant, who teaches dance to kindergarten through fifth grade at P.S. 89 Liberty School in New York City, voices the opinion of many: that with our increasingly sedentary lifestyle choices, children simply *need* to move. "In the past few years, the time the children spend in front of screens has exponentially risen," she says in an interview, "and so the need just for unstructured play is very great." Gallant's creative movement approach to teaching dance provides such unstructured play.

But learning to dance also introduces structure and discipline—not the kind that is imposed on us, but a deep-rooted response, an innate sense of orderliness and harmony. Appreciation of the visual arts, both sculpture and painting, is spurred by dance training; dance aids recognition of form, balance, and line. Dance also encourages an awareness of the rhythm in all of life and our participation in that rhythm. Bertram Ross, a former principal member of the Martha Graham Dance Company and a teacher at the Graham school in New York, exclaimed during one class: "Go to the country, go to the park, take your shoes off, and run through the grass!" He encouraged a reconnection with nature in order to understand the movement he was demonstrating. Animals in the wild do not overeat or oversleep; they live in harmony with their nature. It could be argued that a lack of discipline is a sign of imbalance, or, conversely, that a balanced life is a disciplined life. When we are not in harmony with our nature, it is as if we close the door to our inner promptings. We stay up too late at night, feel groggy in the morning, drink too much coffee, and then are perhaps wired up and prone to rash decisions. We are out of balance and may act in an undisciplined manner. Finding balance can come in many forms. For some it's that trip to the country, taking shoes off, and feeling grass caressing the toes. For others, it's going to a dance class.

Much has been written about the "high" that runners experience during a vigorous race. In a subtler and perhaps a more complete way, dancers also experience a transcendent sensation. After a good class all worries seem manageable, all problems solvable. During a difficult period in my life, my mother once said to me as I was leaving for class, "Go seek your oblivion." She was right. Class provided solace and grounding; in class I had a measure of control, and the physical exertion was in itself cleansing.

At many performing arts high schools, the dance students are the most disciplined members of the school community. Typically they have a high grade-point average, are responsible about handing in their homework on time, and are courteous and considerate. They form a close—but not closed—community and are supportive of each other. Although some will not pursue a career in dance after graduation, all invest a maximum of effort in their technical improvement and their understanding of the art form.

The Greeks knew the value of dance; not only did they dance in worship and ritual, but they also made dance a part of the training of athletes and warriors. Through exercise comes control and awareness, and through control comes a heightened sense of physicality, coordination, and grace. In the heyday of the European Renaissance all of Europe danced, and its courts laid the foundation of today's ballet. After the dark Medieval era, when asceticism, self-denial, self-flagellation, and hairshirts had been thought to bring one closer to God, humankind was again free to extol the pleasure of well-being through movement. Later, at the seventeenth-century French court of Louis XIV, courtly manners were polished through the study of dance and deportment. In 1661 Louis established the Academie Royale de la Danse, marking the beginning of the separation between professionals and amateurs. Technique developed and was codified, a sophisticated notation system was developed, and treatises on training were written.

Dance training has an expanded presence in our current age of heightened awareness of and emphasis on physical fitness. Many people either take up dancing for the first time or return to it in their adulthood. They appreciate the toning and control that dance fosters, enjoy the soothing predictability of the lesson structure, and can let their imaginations soar to the rhythms of the classical music of the ballet class or the driving pulse of a modern or jazz dance class.

HISTORICAL OVERVIEW

Of the ballet, modern, tap, and jazz dance styles, ballet is the first to have developed training methods. The rules of the classical ballet technique are based on the motions that are natural to human beings. For example, when we walk, as the right foot comes forward the left arm swings forward. From this natural action came ballet's use of opposition. Balance and the need to maximize the push off the floor in jumps made us appreciate how the weight of the body affects all movement. This knowledge resulted in dancers' associating positions of the head and arms with specific postures or movements of the legs in order to facilitate or counterbalance motions. The use of turnout (rotating the leg outward from the hip) came about when it was discovered that turning out the toes allowed for a variety of steps to be executed that were otherwise either impossible or ungainly, such as the entrechat, a jump in which the legs bypass each other in a rapid beating motion. Louis XIV is reputed to have mastered the entrechat six (the legs bypass each other three times during the jump). A popular explanation for the renaming of the entrechat trois, a single beating of the legs, is that when Louis could no longer perform the more difficult entrechat six, the entrechat trois became known as "royale" in order not to offend the king. The early technique focused on intricate footwork accompanied by graceful movements in the upper body, head, and arms.

Costumes into the eighteenth century were rather cumbersome, as they followed the fashion of the day. Marie Camargo (1710–1770) scandalized her public by shortening her skirt to reveal her ankle and thus show off the cabriole jumps and entrechats that she has mastered. These steps had previously been performed only by male dancers, whose costumes permitted a fuller view of the body as well as a broader range of motion. Camargo's rebellious gesture has assured her place in the history books, but more importantly, she opened the door for female dancers to experience the whole breadth of the technique.

During the eighteenth century, dance's vocabulary of motion relied on the steps used in court dances. Dance teachers experimented with movement to find new steps or sequences, which they then used in the composition of dances. Dancers were often their own choreographers, and they favored steps in which they excelled. For example, if a dancer pirouetted easily, he or she practiced turns and incorporated them into his or her compositions, utilizing them more than other motions; thus dancers became known for specific feats. As dance steps increased in complexity the gap between the vocabulary of the court dances and professional dance widened, and the need to train dancers arose. A set vocabulary for training emerged, and exercises involving the barre developed as a prelude for work in the center, which became the basis for a choreographic vocabulary.

Renowned dancer Carlo Blasis (1797–1878) was considered the most influential teacher of his day. In 1830 he published *The Code of Terpsichore, a Treatise on the Art of Dancing*. In this book Blasis outlines several types of motions still performed today, and discusses the function of the exercises in limbering up for performance. These exercises form the base of the classical ballet technique.

By the romantic era, from the 1820s, all dancers underwent Blasis's recommended training regimen. Marie Taglioni (1804–1884), the epitome of the romantic ballerina, was taught by her father, Filippo Taglioni (1777–1871). She often fainted from exhaustion by the end of the two-hour classes that he devised for her.

Ethereality and lightness were some of the essential characteristics of a romantic ballerina. In order to enhance those qualities, female dancers began to rise fleetingly on their toes. From this physical innovation the pointe shoe developed, with its sturdy tip to protect the toes and its pliable yet strong inner sole to support the arch. By the second half of the nineteenth century, dancing on pointe had become an important facet of the ballerina's technique.

Ballet technique is ultimately adaptable to the character of the people performing it. Thus in the late nineteenth century, Italian dancers were known for their speed and dexterity in turning, the French for their nobility, the Danish for the lightness of their jumps. Ballet masters of the nineteenth century traveled extensively, which accounts for the dissemination of ballet technique as well as its basic homogeneity. This tradition of travel has persisted to our day, ensuring the continued sharing of ideas and making dancers true citizens of the world.

Russia had long admired the arts of Western Europe, especially those of the French. Russia routinely imported dancing masters both to teach at the Imperial School and to produce ballets. The man credited with the rise and preeminence of the Russian ballet is Marius Petipa (1818–1910), who came to Russia in 1847 as a dancer and was appointed ballet master and choreographer in 1862. He held the position of choreographer until his retirement in 1903. Under his leadership the foundation of the classical repertory was established, and the rules and usages of the ballet vocabulary were firmly fixed. Two more notable styles influenced the emergence of the Russian style: the Danish School, represented by Christian

Johannsson (1817–1903), who, after a distinguished dancing career, became chief teacher at the Mariinsky in 1860; and the Italian School, represented by Enrico Cecchetti (1850–1928), who taught in Russia from 1892. One of the predominant features of Russian folk dancing is the expressiveness of the arms and upper body. This feature was incorporated into the balletic vocabulary and gave the Russian style its particular character. Because expressiveness of the upper body relies on the strength and flexibility of the torso, the basic exercises practiced in class needed to address this issue. Nicolai Legat (1869–1937), teacher and theorist, embodied this blending of styles upon which the Russian School is based. Later, Agrippina Vaganova (1879–1951) based the method of teaching in Russian schools on Legat's theories.

In 1908 the Russian impresario Serge Diaghilev (1872–1929) brought to Paris the production of the opera *Boris Godunov* by Mussorgsky. The overwhelming success of this production led to successive Russian seasons in Paris. Although the initial season featured opera, not ballet, the French public was especially impressed with the dancers whom Diaghilev had assembled from the ranks of the Mariinsky and Bolshoi ballets, including Vaslav Nijinsky and Tamara Karsavina. Both Cecchetti and Legat were employed at different times as ballet masters for Diaghilev's company. Les Ballets Russes de Diaghilev, as the company was eventually known, was the instrument by which interest in dance was rekindled in the West, leading to a renaissance of the art form not only in Europe but in the United States as well.

Previously, toward the end of the nineteenth century in Europe, dance had experienced a decline. Ballet had become a frivolous display that relied more on the charm and youth of the dancers to attract the public than on artistic merit.

Some artists rebelled against what they perceived as ballet's mockery, denouncing it as mere form with no content. Isadora Duncan (1878–1927) dared to dance barefoot in a light tunic that allowed her to move freely and revealed the lines of her body, and she developed her own expressive style of movement. Although Duncan did not attract American audiences at the beginning of her career, Europe, especially Germany and Russia, welcomed and admired her. Her ideas prompted a reevaluation of the established practices in the dance world, and she greatly influenced a young choreographer at the Imperial School, Mikhail Fokine (1880–1942). In his approach to ballet choreography, Fokine became highly critical of the three-act ballets so popular during Petipa's tenure. He sought a freer use of the classical technique, and he was able to express his bold ideas as the first choreographer of Diaghilev's innovative productions.

By the beginning of the twentieth century, classical ballet was putting down roots in American soil. Anna Pavlova (1881–1931) introduced audiences to the art form by touring extensively in both South and North America. Ballet schools were established in Philadelphia, Chicago, and New York in the early part of the century. In 1934 George Balanchine (1904–1983) started the famous School of American Ballet in New York, and around that time Ninette de Valois (1898–2001) formed what was to become the Royal Ballet.

Also in the early 1900s, modern dance emerged as an idea whose time had come. In both the United States and Germany, dancers began to experiment with the new movement fostered by Duncan's work. They turned their backs on the constraints of ballet technique, feeling that dance should express emotions and ideas without resorting to stereotyped gestures. The German artist Mary Wigman (1886–1973) had a great impact on American modern dance through her pupil Hanya Holm (1893–1992), who came to New York in 1931 and nurtured generations of modern dancers. In 1915 in Los Angeles, Ruth St. Denis (1879–1968) and Ted Shawn (1891–1972) opened a school dedicated to the study of their style of modern dance, and started a company known as Denishawn. St. Denis was greatly influenced by Eastern dance, and her choreographic choices reflected that interest. In 1933 Shawn broke from the partnership and established an all-male dance troupe, which toured extensively and was instrumental in overcoming the prejudice against male dancers. Many of the future innovators of modern dance studied at Denishawn and danced in the company. These include Martha Graham (1899–1991), Doris Humphrey (1895–1958), and Charles Weidman (1901–1975). When Graham formed her own company, she began to develop a training method to support her choreographic ideas. Her central concept was torso contraction and release as the initiator for all action. Her movements were often angular and percussive, and her early works were influenced by Freudian symbolism and mythology. Doris Humphrey based her approach to movement on the concepts of fall and recovery. Her dances were often fluid and ecstatic. In 1928 Humphrey and Weidman formed their own company, for which Weidman created many works, mostly in a light satirical vein.

These early pioneers spawned a new generation of dancers who shaped the profile of modern dance to our day. Among them were José Limón (1908–1972), who had a lifelong association with Humphrey, and Merce Cunningham (1919–2009), who danced with Martha Graham before forming his own company in 1952, where he was able to work out his own style of isolated movement in often aleatory compositions. The second generation of innovators included Alwin Nikolais (1912–1993), Erick Hawkins (1909–1994), Sybil Shearer (1918–2005), Murray Louis (b. 1926), and Paul Taylor (b. 1930). They were categorized as nonliteral choreographers. Nikolais and Louis formed the Nikolais-Louis Dance Theatre Lab and produced many experimental works, their central premise being that "the province of art is to explore the inner mechanisms and extra dimensional areas of life."[1] Hawkins, a leading dancer in Martha Graham's company, broke away to form a partnership with the musician Lucia Dlugoszewski (1925–2000). Together they created many dances based on Hawkins's philosophy of the immediacy of experience: dance happens in the now. Shearer danced with the Humphrey-Weidman company and eventually settled in Illinois, where she established a studio and theatre. She created highly individualist works that relied on energetic action coupled with a serene minimalism of motion. Taylor studied modern dance with Graham and Limón, and ballet with Anthony Tudor and Margaret Craske. His dynamic choreographic style is eclectic and can be nonliteral, then verge on the classical.

The list of innovative twentieth-century choreographers is too long to complete here. However, we cannot stop before mentioning Alvin Ailey (1931–1989), a student of Lester Horton's (1906–1953) Native American-influenced style. Ailey brought a blues/spiritual infused African American presence to modern dance choreography. Twyla Tharp (b. 1942) studied with Graham, Nikolais, Cunningham, and Taylor. Her choreography is performed by major ballet as well as modern dance companies, and she had a fruitful

---

[1] Murray Louis, "The Contemporary Dance Theatre of Alwin Nikolais," *Dance Observer* 27:1 (Jan. 1960), 5–6.

association with Mikhail Baryshnikov (b. 1948) during his tenure as artistic director of the American Ballet Theatre. Also of note, Mark Morris (b. 1956) developed a balletic contemporary style often interpreting classical music, derived from his early folk dance training and from studies with Hannah Kahn, Laura Dean, and Eliot Feld, among others. Many black concert dancers of this century began their training in modern dance, and as choreographers they were able to return to their roots in the creation of powerfully moving dance works. Among the most notable are Pearl Primus (1919–1994), Katherine Dunham (1912–2006), and Ailey.

To this day, modern dance encourages individualistic expression. Although innovators have established recognized styles, modern dance choreographers often break away from their mentors to discover their own way of moving and to build a personal vocabulary of choreographic movement.

The jazz dance form is considered a truly American expression, with origins in the dances of African slaves in America. Despite the Slave Law of 1740, which forbade the playing of drums as well as other instruments, the slaves continued to dance. They adapted to the law by accompanying their dances with clapping hands and banjos as well as the sounds of stamping or shuffling feet. Tap dancing developed from these rhythms. The Irish clog dancers who came to America in the middle of the nineteenth century adopted this tapping and modified it with their own rhythmic combinations. Early pioneers of jazz dance included Bill "Bojangles" Robinson (1878–1949), the Nicholas brothers, and Honi Coles. Savion Glover, Lane Alexander, and Brenda Bufalino are among those who have contributed to a revitalization of tap dance in the early twenty-first century.

Jazz and tap dancing began to appear in films in the 1920s, and both established their supremacy in theatrical entertainments such as the extravaganzas of Busby Berkeley (1895–1976) and the beautiful dances choreographed by Agnes de Mille (1909–1993) for musical theatre productions such as *Oklahoma* (1943). Fred Astaire (1899–1987) is probably the most admired performer of tap dance. His elegant style and exquisite subtleties set the example for the many dancers who followed in his footsteps, like Gene Kelly (1912–1996).

Jazz relies heavily on both classical and modern techniques for the content and sequencing of its warm-up exercises, adapting them to reflect its particularities—percussive motions, the use of a broadly opened hand, emphasis on isolation of movement, and a free approach to turnout (using turned out or parallel legs as the need arises). Jazz has as many styles as modern dance. It has developed its own warm-up exercises, the choice of which usually reflects the bias of the instructor or choreographer. For example, a choreographer whose training was primarily in modern dance will incorporate the concepts of that technique into his or her teaching methods in jazz.

It is only in the last sixty years (this development was very slow) that dance, including modern dance, has taken on its present athletic profile. Until the 1940s legs were rarely lifted above 90 degrees in extensions, and turnout of the legs was closer to 45 degrees than to 90 degrees. At the Paris Opera Ballet in the early 1950s, only two young ballerinas could achieve extensions close to 160 degrees; their arabesques left observers gaping. Josette Amiel and Claude Bessy, brunette and blonde respectively, were often paired together in ballets in which their accomplishments could be highlighted by the choreographer.

This newfound ability to extend the legs at this dizzying height had a profound effect on ballet technique. Not only does it require more flexibility to execute leg extensions above 90 degrees, but it also requires more strength and cooperation from the muscles of the torso. Classroom exercises reflected this new thrust by emphasizing flexibility and extension. The entire line of the body became more extended. The strength that dancers developed through this emphasis led to the pyrotechnics of the current age.

The wisdom of ballet's sequencing of exercises is now recognized by proponents of other techniques. Each technique addresses the need to stretch and strengthen, and each applies its concepts to centre work in its own way. In a dance class every joint of the body should be gradually warmed, and all muscles stretched and strengthened. The structure of a modern dance class follows a similar pattern: after the initial warm-up exercises, balance, turns, jumps, and falls are practiced in combinations in the center and across the floor.

Ballet training has also come to be widely recognized and appreciated by dancers and choreographers as necessary for the development of a technical background. Ballet can be safely performed by the very young, and it most efficiently keeps a trained body in shape. The Alvin Ailey School, an enclave of modern dance, requires its summer students to take five ballet classes, two modern dance classes, and one jazz class a week, and for Hubbard Street Dance Chicago, whose repertory is stylistically eclectic, the daily company class is ballet.

It is very important to make a distinction between training methods and choreography. Training is the means by which a dancer arrives at a level of proficiency commensurate with her or his potential, and thereafter not only keeps in shape but has an opportunity to push the boundaries and achieve an ever-subtler execution of motions. Choreography, on the other hand, is the use, usually by an individual but sometimes by a group working collaboratively, of a dance vocabulary to express an idea, tell a story, or explore the dynamics of motion. Most dance companies have a specific style within each discipline—ballet, modern, jazz, or tap. A company's style may be developed over a period of years and is usually guided by the vision of an individual, like the Royal Ballet in London under the leadership of Ninette de Valois, or the Joffrey Ballet with Robert Joffrey (1930–1989) or, later, Gerald Arpino (1923–2008) at the helm. The training style may be narrow, like those initially developed at the New York City Ballet and the Martha Graham School, or it may be more inclusive, like that of the American Ballet Theatre, whose repertoire includes works by choreographers from Petipa to William Forsythe. Modern choreographers tend to develop individualistic styles that distinguish them from other choreographers, while ballet choreographers generally remain within the confines, more or less rigidly defined, of the ballet vocabulary.

Most dancers excel in one technique and concentrate their energies on that discipline in order to perfect it. Nevertheless, the study of ballet is central to improving technical proficiency for all dancers.

A preballet class incorporates some of the elements of creative move-
ment. It also introduces some basic classical ballet positions and motions.
Students from the School of Madison Ballet, Madison, Wisconsin. © 2015
Maureen Janson

2

DANCE TRAINING

WHEN WE ENGAGE IN ANY physical activity in a consistent manner over a period of time, we encourage the development of synaptic connections in the brain. These connections allow new moves to become part of our vocabulary of motion, just as crawling, walking, and running become part of our automatic response. These learned systems share a common feature: a broadening of the base of habitual actions that we can use consciously and with intent. When we talk of technique, we refer to training methods that employ a patterning process that is the repetition of specific motions until these motions become part of our physical vocabulary.

Basic motions are the building blocks of any dance technique and are usually selected because they support the style desired. Style can be understood as the result of choices made during training. For example, a person who has played golf for a long time is not necessarily good at tennis, because each sport employs specific actions that apply only peripherally to other sports. More often than not, style and technique are so intimately bound from the earliest stages of dance training that it is difficult to say where technique ends and style begins. Balinese dance, for example, has characteristic hand gestures and a rhythmic pattern that distinguishes it from African dance, in which the hand gestures are much freer in form and the rhythmic patterns are more dynamic. Both dance forms have specific and distinct methods of instruction.

Techniques build vocabulary by going from the simple to the complex. Basic motions are repeated over and over again, and eventually these motions can be linked into combinations. At first, combinations are limited to two or three basic motions; as the student progresses the combinations become more complex, although they will still be comprised of the basic motions. When a method of teaching moves too quickly into the complex (a series of motions linked together) and overlooks the learning of basic motions in the very early stages of training, the building blocks, or steps of the technique, are not delineated in the student's mind and are therefore not clear in the execution of the motions.

The term "primary techniques" refers to those methods that teach basic motions over a long enough period of time to allow the synaptic connections in the brain to be formed. Another crucial component of dance training is the developed ability to maintain posture in some areas of the body while performing energetic actions with other parts of the body. This stabilization is essential to controlled movement. Both ballet and Graham techniques employ this concept. A primary technique will also facilitate the learning of another technique. For example, a dancer who has integrated a primary technique learns other styles faster than one without training or with poor training. Theoretically, any technique can be primary if it develops specific motions as the basic building blocks of that particular dance form.

Ballet as a primary technique for would-be dancers has developed definitive teaching tools, both in its choice of exercises and in their sequencing. In good ballet training (not all ballet teaching adheres to the principles of the art form), for at least the first two years the student holds the arms in second position (to the side) while concentrating on the motions of the legs. Combining the movements of the arms and legs is very gradual. After focusing on leg motions, the student performs arm movement sequences while standing in position—that is, in isolation from leg motions. Later on the two elements will be performed together, but only after the path of the arms and the path of the legs have been established separately. In ballet, "isolation" consists of inhibiting certain responses; the student learns not to lift the shoulder when lifting the arm, or not to shift the pelvis when lifting a leg. Each exercise is performed in its most basic form until the integrity of the isolated motion has been established. The position of the arm and the posture of the body are especially critical, because conscious control of these body parts is crucial to the correct execution of all motions.

Educational systems have pitted creativity and formal elements of technique against one another. Some instructors seem to believe that the mere introduction of technique will compromise, if not kill, creativity. However, this arduous process is not an end in itself; it is only the means. Technique represents the acquisition of tools that will allow the artist to freely utilize imagination and creativity. We learn technique to be able to forget it, transcend it, and communicate fully our intent. Creativity needs tools to help fashion ideas, to bring them into concreteness. Art begins with a conscious intent. Dance is a most intimate art because it uses the body in its creation. Ignoring the technical aspects of an art form can deny the benefit of an established vocabulary that inevitably provides an underpinning for originality.

The purpose of dance training is to acquire technique. One definition of technique is "a method of accomplishing a desired aim." The aim of dance instruction is to train the body into an expressive and responsive instrument. A violinmaker selects the wood, prepares it, shapes it, fashions the pieces together, polishes it, and, finally, attaches the strings. Only then is the instrument ready to be played. Early dance training can be compared to the building of a violin. Specific methods and tools facilitate the task within each stage. For example, the pieces will not be glued together before each one is the correct shape, nor the strings attached before the glue has set.

In dance, the building of the instrument is dependent on our physical and mental development. We must learn to walk before we can run. As we learn to walk, we develop habits that will serve the act of running more or less efficiently depending on the neuromuscular connections we have established. Although scientific research is providing us information about various aspects of our being that were mysteries a century ago, the human body has not evolved at that same pace. We are still limited by a rate of growth both mental and physical. No matter what teaching methods we use, we still cannot expect a two-year-old to grasp concepts of higher mathematics. If the aim of taking dance classes is the acquisition of skills, then the progression of training suggested in this book can be seen as a logical, developmental process designed to serve the purpose.

Initially, creative movement introduces children to nonformal dance. Ballet, modern dance, and tap can be studied concurrently to develop formal movement patterns, rhythmic and spatial awareness, and a creative approach to motion. Jazz is not a technique but a style. Jazz incorporates aspects of ballet, modern, African, and tap and modifies them stylistically into a dynamic dance form. Jazz may be compared to musical theatre dance, which is not a discipline unto itself. A musical theatre artist studies dance, voice, and acting lessons to perfect skills in all of those areas before putting them all together and applying them to the musical theatre repertory.

What one chooses to do with the instrument one has built depends on individual taste, preference, and, ultimately, choreography.

THE EARLY YEARS: CREATIVE MOVEMENT AND PREBALLET

Creative movement and preballet are both based on the idea of providing physical activity for children who are too young for formal technical training. (Before age seven or eight children's bones are too soft, their muscular connections insufficiently established, and their attention spans too short to focus on technical details.) Creative movement is sometimes taught by modern dance teachers and preballet by classically trained teachers. Some schools teach both, beginning with creative movement for the very young and then moving on to preballet for a slightly more technical approach.

The activities devised to enhance movement awareness may be based on the Swiss music teacher Emile Jaques-Dalcroze's (1865–1950) system of movement. Although this system was developed to train young musicians, not dancers, to express rhythms through movement, it is a wonderful system for all children who need to develop coordination between what is seen or heard and a specific physical response.

Some modern dance methods also allow full participation by very young children when they do not stress formal motion. The child is free to express feelings and ideas with movement in a nonjudgmental environment. Improvisational techniques are also a good beginning for children, stressing group activity and an awareness of both space and other people.

Creative movement classes generally place emphasis on shape, space, and response to different sounds or rhythms. The classes challenge the child's imagination, heightening awareness both of the body and how it moves through space, and of relationships to others who share that space and create patterns. They achieve this goal through the use of musical games, storytelling in movement, and mimicry of our natural environment—clouds, rain, waves, flowers, trees, animals. They also sharpen perception of spatial relationships as well as shapes and dynamics. Through these activities and others—such as gentle stretching and gross motor-control motions, like skipping and marching—children learn to give physical expression to their visualizations, and to develop motor-control coordination.

The teacher of creative movement is typically responsive to and supportive of the shapes and motions the child creates, and encourages the discovery of new shapes or alternate ways of moving.

A preballet class incorporates some of the elements of creative movement. It also introduces some basic classical ballet positions and motions without emphasizing their technical aspects.

While both types of classes develop flexibility, coordination, and sensitivity to music and rhythm, children also discover the pleasure of kinetic self-expression within a framework that challenges their perceptions. Ideally, the structure of the class allows for enough freedom of expression to give children a sense that they are participating in a discovery, not that there are right or wrong responses to directions. This approach enhances the child's self-image and develops self-confidence along with physical and spatial skills.

BEGINNING FORMAL TRAINING: BALLET

Ballet enlarges, formalizes, and redirects the movement vocabulary that is naturally available to us—walking, running, twisting, bending, flailing the arms, kicking the legs, and shaking the head. Through the repetition of simple motions that increase in complexity as the technique is integrated, ballet builds a musculature that is both strong and flexible and increases the range of motion of the joints. It fosters a balanced alignment and good posture, and it allows children to develop at an early age the necessary coordination and movement skills that will enable them to respond and adapt to other movement styles. Ballet is a primary technique because it teaches a basic movement vocabulary and relies on the stabilization concept for the execution of that vocabulary. However, it should not be introduced to children before age seven at the earliest. Many schools offer tap classes for students in this age group. Tap promotes coordination, an acute sense of rhythmic patterns, and, above all, it is fun—an attribute not always found in ballet. In addition, like ballet, tap encourages the retention of movement patterns and thus aids in the development of kinetic memory (the ability to remember specific movements and sequences of movements). While modern dance also addresses these concepts, it is not generally in a studio curriculum for ages seven to twelve, although it is increasingly becoming an option.

In a ballet class, initial practice is limited to approximately five of the ten distinct exercises that are performed at the barre. As the body gets stronger, further exercises are introduced until all ten are known and practiced. Along with the exercises, the five positions of the feet and the arm positions are learned. Basic jumps are also introduced.

These exercises are basic because they involve fundamental movements that establish pathways for all later motions. Motions of the leg are stretching the straight leg, flexing the ankle or the knee, flexing the leg at the hip joint, moving the leg to the front, back, and side, and circular motion at the hip joint and at the knee. Motions of the arms are front, side, and overhead. Positions of the head are straight forward, tilted, turned, and circular. Similarly, the basic jumps develop the action that will be necessary for all jumps. (There are only five ways to jump: from two feet to two feet, from two feet to one foot, from one foot to two feet, from one foot to the other, and from one foot to the same one foot).

The traditional barre practice begins with plié, the bending of the knees and flexion at the hip and ankle joints in the five positions. Young beginners practice only three of the five. There are two versions of the plié: demi (half) and grand (deep). Initially only the demi plié is practiced, and generally in the following positions with the feet turned out to 45 degrees:

First position: feet turned out and heel to heel.
Second position: feet apart, to the side, separated by about
 a foot and a half.

Third position: the heel of one foot placed in front of the other in a tight position.

Positions introduced later in the training process, when the musculature can cope with a greater degree of turnout of the feet, are:

Fourth position: feet placed in front of one another in an open position, separated by about 12 inches.

Fifth position: feet placed heel-to-toe in front of one another.

The remaining exercises are:

Battement tendu (stretching): the leg is stretched out to front, side, or back, the toes pointing but never leaving the floor.

Battement tendu jeté (throwing motion) or *degagé* (disengagement, terminology of the Italian School): the leg is stretched out in the same way as in a battement tendu, but the toes come off the ground to a height of about 45 degrees.

Rond de jambe par terre (circular motion): with the toes never leaving the floor, the leg describes a half-circle from front to back and back to front, passing through first position.

Battement frappé (hitting or striking): a percussive motion from the knee down. The working leg's heel is placed on the ankle of the supporting leg, and the leg is then stretched out in a fast motion (initially to toes touching the floor, subsequently to a 45-degree angle off the floor) to the front, side, or back. Beginners master the side position first.

The above exercises comprise the vocabulary for the first year of training. The other exercises are as follows:

Battement fondu (melting motion): begins with a plié on the supporting leg while the other is placed in a retiré position (knee bent, toes touching the supporting leg in front or back). Proceeds to a full extension in the air while the supporting leg is straightened.

Rond de jambe en l'air (circle of the leg in the air): the leg is lifted to the side, eventually to 90 degrees off the floor, and the lower leg describes a small circle either outward or inward (outward is a motion from back to front, and inward is from front to back). The action is limited to the knee joint.

Developpé (unfolding): the working leg is lifted to a high extension, passing through a retiré position.

Petit battement sur le cou de pied (little beating on the ankle): the heel of the foot performing the action is placed on the ankle of the supporting leg and strikes the ankle back and front. The action is limited to the knee joint.

Grand battement (big leg lifts): the working leg is lifted straight upward as high as it will go and returns to a closed position before the next battement.

The terminology for the positions of the arms varies greatly from school to school, but there are only two fundamental positions. In the first, the arms are down, slightly rounded, and held in front of the body; the same position can be lifted to a place just in front of the sternum, first position, and also above the head, fifth position. In the second position, the arms are held to the side just below shoulder height. All other positions are derived from these basic ones.

These exercises prepare both the musculature and the brain to perform all the potential movements of the vocabulary and to respond efficiently to directions. Moreover, the basic exercises lend themselves to manipulation; any number of variations on the theme can be devised to emphasize a concept or introduce a notion.

After a barre exercise warm-up, the ballet class continues with work in the center of the floor. Initially the vocabulary is limited to a handful of basic steps. Eventually the students will perform some exercises from the barre repeated in short sequences; these may include turns. They will then perform adagios (slow, sustained motions of legs in extensions) to test balance and coordination. Then come the jumps, first small jumps close to the floor, then big ones across the floor.

When building a house, one must establish a level and sound foundation to ensure the soundness of the rest of the structure. Ballet provides this foundation for dance. It does not exclude the introduction of modern dance concepts, which many teachers provide after the basics have been established. Young dancers are engaged in enlarging their movement vocabulary and their awareness of movement potential. They are building a house in which they will live the rest of their lives.

TAP DANCE TRAINING

Tap focuses on the sounds and rhythms that can be obtained through the control of dynamics and energy. The knees and ankle joints are relaxed enough to allow free motion of the feet. Initially children learn basic rhythms by using either the heel or the toe to produce the sounds. Eventually, more complex rhythms can be obtained with accompanying motions of the legs and body, which may include leaps and turns. Dexterity, quickness, and a relaxed stance are encouraged. Although some formal arm positions may accompany the tapping, they are open to a freer interpretation than ballet positions.

A tap class includes the practice of specific rhythmic patterns and may end in short routines, in which the material learned can be applied creatively.

MODERN DANCE TRAINING

It is much harder to categorize the training methods of modern dance because it has always been motivated by an individual need for self-expression. Far more voices exist in modern dance than in ballet training, which precludes a universal measurability. For example, the Humphrey-Weidman technique is spatially oriented, whereas the Graham technique is based on the experience of one's own center. Although a choreographer may devise original training movement sequences that lead logically to utility in choreography, there are some features that are common to a majority of styles. Some of these features are:

> The concept of the center as the place where all movement originates, as well as motions that are performed off-center.
> The use of breath to initiate movement.

The contraction, a hollowing inward of the abdominals until the spine curves, and the release, which straightens the body out of the contraction.

Increased use of torso movement.

The use of the parallel positioning of the legs, and the study of how this affects extending the leg away from the floor.

An extensive use of prone movements.

The concept of fall and recovery as initiator of motion, and the study of specific falls that illustrate this concept.

The willingness to question any rule.

A modern dance class may begin with exercises on the floor (Graham technique) or standing up. The standing exercises include motions already familiar from the ballet class but executed with the legs both in parallel and turned-out positions, such as bending the knees in a variety of positions (legs together and apart), often including a contraction and release; stretching the leg along the floor to full extension (tendu); taking that motion off the floor (jeté); a variety of stretches of the torso together with arm motions that can be either swinging or sustained; and a variety of high leg extensions with tilts off-center and contractions (adagio). This section of the class often ends with high kicks (grand battement). A variety of turns and leaps across the floor follow. Usually the teacher will choreograph a movement phrase to be learned and practiced.

The conceptual method of modern dance introduces the dancer to formal elements of movement, such as shape, effort, and dynamics. This type of training can begin at an early age. However, when it does not practice basic formal motions, it does not develop the necessary neuromuscular connections that are the basis of technique. As stated earlier, the repetition of simple physical motions that encourage synaptic connections in the brain are central to this development. Nevertheless, a conceptual method of dance training encourages children to use their imagination and to discover movement patterns that are personally expressive.

Modern dance relies heavily on lineage. If a teacher advertises as a Graham teacher, you can expect to learn the technique developed by Martha Graham. Merce Cunningham-trained teachers will be more balletic in their approach without, however, an emphasis on the classical line. Lester Horton influenced a generation of dancers and teachers with a vigorous athletic style. Doris Humphrey developed a fluid style based on fall and recovery, giving in to the pull of gravity and resisting it in turn. José Limón (1908–1972), on the other hand, explored the circularity and connectedness of motion. These are a few of the innovators whose precepts have been accepted and are utilized to a greater or lesser degree by many contemporary modern dancers and teachers.

Between the ages of seven and nine, young dancers can begin the study of Martha Graham technique by way of basic elements. This method demands a great deal of control and awareness. It relies on dynamics and concepts that require an intellectual as well as a physical response. This type of control and introspection are best introduced when a child is old enough to engage these skills and can draw full benefit from this technique. By age ten, students can be more fully able to grasp this technique.

Graham devised an extensive vocabulary of floor exercises that includes contraction, release, and spiraling of the torso with accompanying head, arm, and leg motions. These are rigorous movements and presume a measure of control of the spinal column and hip joint. The Graham class starts sitting on the floor to execute a series of formal exercises with emphasis on the torso's ability to contract, release, and spiral. The legs are stretched and bent and the instep flexed or pointed, depending on the exercise. The arm and head positions are an integral part of each motion. The next section of the class may include some of the standing exercises mentioned earlier. The class ends with turns and leaps across the studio. The progression of training, like ballet, has a tracking process that introduces the child to certain movements first, and progresses as the child is able grasp more. A Graham class is even more regimented than a ballet class, and true exponents of the technique do not waver from the structure or the content.

It's often easy to confuse choreographic merits with training methods. The latter is our focus here. Many formally trained dancers have moved away from their primary technique and gone on to create original movement in their choreography. Their choreographic output and style should not be mistaken for a training method.

In dance today, modern dance and ballet techniques are not mutually exclusive. Ballet technique is valued by modern dancers for its ability to keep the body tuned. Although some modern movements, such as the deep contraction, have no counterpart in the balletic training vocabulary, they are often used choreographically in ballet. Both techniques require a strong sense of centeredness. Isadora Duncan considered the center to be located at the solar plexus, the area around the lower sternum. She believed that all movement comes from that center. *Center* refers to the general area of the belly, which is, in actuality, the body's center of gravity. An awareness of that part of the body is an essential aspect of all motion and is strongly emphasized in the modern technique. It helps to enhance the strength of the spine as well as access the deep muscles of the torso. Moreover, motions that involve prone positions on the floor have been freely adopted by contemporary ballet choreographers. Today's dancer is best served by being versed in both techniques to be able to respond fully to all choreographic demands.

JAZZ TRAINING

Many schools teach jazz to young children as a primary technique, borrowing the training vocabulary from ballet and modern. In many cases, jazz dance is presented as a hybrid along with hip-hop and popular dance styles. If the training method addresses a basic movement vocabulary as well as the stabilizing concept and does not overly stress the learning of routines, students may achieve technical proficiency through jazz dance studies. However, if learning routines predominates, students will not have the opportunity to develop solid technical knowledge.

As in modern dance, there are many jazz styles, ranging from the overtly sexual to the powerfully dynamic. The sensuality inherent in jazz and hip-hop movement is an adult expression, its movements having evolved on mature bodies whose spines and hip sockets are fully developed. Children's bodies, still in the process of growth, are not equipped to cope with the motions, often sharply percussive, that the style demands. Although in jazz and hip-hop the concept of isolation holds a central place, within technical dance training it does not seem to foster the kind of stability that ballet and Graham techniques encourage.

A degree of control needs to be established before jazz isolations can be executed safely. Meribeth Kisner-Griffin, former artistic director of Chi-Town Jazz Dance, is emphatic about a progression of training that begins with ballet as the foundation. She generally would not admit students in her class before they were age sixteen and had acquired a solid grounding in ballet technique.

Jazz classes rely heavily on the movement vocabulary of both ballet and modern dance in the formulation of their exercises. Most of the exercises already described here are part of the jazz class, which may start with dancers standing at the barre or in the center depending on the preference of the teacher. The motions are usually more percussive than in either ballet or modern. The hands are often splayed, fingers strongly extended. The structure of the class is, again, similar to that in the other two techniques. After the warm-up exercises students learn shorter or longer combinations of motions, often called routines, which include turns and leaps.

The study of modern and ballet techniques enables the student to adapt quickly to the requirements of jazz, but the converse is seldom true. The student who starts dance training with jazz lessons has greater difficulties adapting to the requirements of the other two disciplines and sometimes cannot overcome the partiality of that early training. However, children enjoy the kinetic aspects of jazz and generally find the style more accessible than either ballet or modern. Nevertheless, the wise parent will keep the ice cream for the end of the meal, after the vegetables and protein have provided the nourishment necessary for the body's growth. Jazz studies should ideally begin after age fifteen, when the musculature and the brain patterns have had a chance to develop.

The ideal sequence of studies is:

Age	Class
4–8	Creative movement, preballet
7–10	Ballet, tap, modern
10–14	Ballet, tap, modern (Graham)
15–18	Ballet, tap, modern, jazz/hip-hop

This sequence is by no means a blueprint; the ages are approximate, and late starters can sometimes follow an accelerated course of studies. Additionally, after some basic technique has been acquired, the child may choose to devote more time to a particular form. A teacher should advocate a logical choice of dance disciplines depending on the student's age, as well as a logical progression through each discipline's curriculum. Before age seven or eight, a nontechnical approach will provide a good introduction to dance through creative movement or preballet classes. At age seven or eight, ballet classes can begin to build the necessary physical foundation through the basic motions of the ballet vocabulary. At the same time, tap can provide an extra physical outlet as it sharpens coordination and rhythmic awareness. Additionally, study of conceptual modern dance can continue to foster creativity and imagination. After age thirteen or fourteen, the young dancer can be introduced to the Graham technique, and after age fifteen, to jazz. It is important to recognize that more is not always better. Many schools offer interdisciplinary classes: in one hour students will learn a bit of ballet, a bit of jazz, some tap, and maybe even gymnastics. The children will not be bored; they will be too busy changing shoes! Enough time should be devoted to one activity for students to develop basic awareness and coordination within a discipline; one hour of a specific technique a week will do more than a number of activities combined. In skipping from one activity to another the students lose the advantage of repeating the simple movement patterns that help them develop the capacity to respond to a wide range of movement possibilities, nor will they develop the ability to focus, which is a challenging yet particularly essential part of any learning process.

OTHER DISCIPLINES

Hip-hop and urban dance styles have begun to appear on the class rosters of many studios. These classes generally refer to dance performed to hip-hop music. Derived from street dance, commercialization of hip-hop has increased its popularity as a studio dance form. Hip-hop dance styles vary widely and are sometimes combined with jazz dance technique in a formal class setting. The freestyle nature of this dance style does not lend itself to any sort of foundation that is easily transferable to the foundational structures of ballet and modern dance. Likewise, cultural dance forms, such as Indian, Middle Eastern, African, and Irish Step dance move in and out of popularity among studio offerings. These forms can greatly supplement a solid training, although they are not considered primary techniques.

Sports and gymnastics, although worthwhile activities in and of themselves, do not help a dancer develop technique. However, a child with a natural kinetic intelligence and a sports or gymnastics background may adapt easily to dance requirements once the initial patterning of those disciplines has been modified. Similarly, lifting weights will make you stronger, but will not help you to dance the tango. Many dancers look to these other disciplines as a means of cross-training and enhancing their primary training and dance skills.

STARTING DANCE AS AN ADULT

So far, the schedule describes a student who begins dance at an early age. However, even late beginners can develop good technique. The late teen years are not too late to begin dance training. Boys in particular, who often avoid taking dance classes because of peer pressure and negative stereotypes associated with male dancers, can achieve good results even with a late start. Many professional male ballet dancers did not start until they were in their late teens or even early twenties. Modern dance allows for a more individual line; many modern dancers started dance in their college years and went on to build stellar careers. Much depends on the physical endowment of the person and on his or her desire to dance.

Whether students begin at age seven, ten, twenty, or forty, the progression in learning the technique is the same; the elements to be integrated are the same. If you are a late beginner, anywhere from fifteen years old to seventy, you will understand the movement intellectually faster than an eight-year-old would. Your kinetic response and your musculature, however, will still need to catch up with your understanding.

In my early thirties, I began studying modern dance. Arrogantly, I thought that I was a trained dancer and did not need to attend beginners' classes. I enrolled in an intermediate Graham class and was quickly humbled. The first month was a challenge! I struggled to keep up in a class where the teacher would simply announce the exercise and everyone around me would immediately begin the sequence, while I trailed a beat behind in an attempt to duplicate what I was seeing. Had I gone to a beginners' class, all of these exercises would have been explained, and the process of integration would have been much faster and certainly more pleasant.

Dance is a demanding and complex skill requiring patience and determination for full mastery. All of the muscles are involved in any single motion, either supportively or actively, and coordinating these elements can be initially intimidating. The good news is that a beginners' class will cover the same basic material over a period of time, gradually building proficiency.

Ballet may be daunting because it strives for a particular line or shape. As proficiency grows, our perceptions of the motions change and demand an ever-greater effort to achieve the ideal. The greatest benefit of ballet exercises comes from a correct execution of the motions. At the beginning, students strive to perform a motion without regard to form (e.g., straight knees or pointed toes). But as the motion becomes routine, the mind becomes free to address concerns of form, shape, and effort; students begin to truly enjoy the activity. To arrive at this point takes patience; integration of the basic elements may take a long time. The wonderful thing about ballet is that it lets students progress at their own pace, and it provides the opportunity to correct a variety of problems within the same exercise. For example, in a battement tendu exercise, one student may concentrate on stretching the knees while another works on extending the arch of the instep; someone else may be thinking about keeping the shoulders down with the arm in position. The corrections and directives of the teacher will indicate the areas that both the class and the individual need to address.

Because of modern dance's individualistic nature, taking a trial class with several different teachers may help you select the one that comes closest to what you expect from a dance class. Although greater freedom of interpretation is inherent in the modern technique, the motions practiced in class are usually as specific as those practiced in a ballet class; patience and perseverance are again needed in order to integrate the motions and gain the greatest benefit from the activity.

The enjoyment of dancing need not be limited to people who intend to become professional dancers. Adults, just as much as children, can benefit from the discipline. Most studios offer adult-beginner classes, and when you feel confident with the vocabulary, you can join any number of open classes in professional studios.

In one class for adults, there was a woman who had taken lessons as a child. Ballet class for her was a means of recapturing the magic of her growing-up years. Twice a week, this insurance executive, dressed in her pink tights and little black skirt, became a ballerina again and twirled around with deep concentration and obvious enjoyment. Others came for the exercise and the opportunity to move to beautiful music. Although dance is not an aerobic activity, it brings all the muscles of the body into play, tones them up, and stretches them. Because dance emphasizes balanced alignment, it can help dissipate the stressful activities of the day that create areas of tension in our bodies. Most importantly, it creates a quiet zone for the psyche; for an hour and a half the outside world recedes, leaving us only the motion and the music.

There is no age limit on performing. Many cities have a seniors dance group that performs at nursing homes and hospitals. One of my dance friends was honored by being asked to join such a group in Great Falls, Montana. At thirty, she was the youngest member in the group, whose ages ranged from fifty to seventy. On one memorable occasion, when she was returning from a trip, she was met at the airport by the entire group in full costume. They proceeded to regale her and other passengers to a tap dance from their repertory.

Once a young dancer has progressed beyond the preballet level, more complex movement patterns are introduced. Students from the School of Madison Ballet, Madison, Wisconsin. © 2015 Maureen Janson

3

HOW TO SELECT A TEACHER

AND SCHOOL

IN THE PROCESS OF CHOOSING a school or a teacher, it's wise to bear in mind two ideas: (1) This is not a life decision; (2) This may be a life decision. The first will help you avoid the sense of competition and urgency that often leads to unwise decisions, such as pressuring the child to excel beyond the capacity of her or his age, or choosing a school or teacher for the wrong reasons (it has the biggest enrollment in the area, or it puts on the most lavish recital at the end of the year). The second will guide you to choose wisely a teacher who can instill a sound foundation that will serve your dancer throughout her or his career.

Like most dancers and dance teachers, I am often asked how I started dancing. Initially, there was no thought of my becoming a professional; my mother simply decided that I needed to take ballet classes to conquer my shyness, straighten my legs, and relax my shoulders enough to show that I had a neck.

Among our acquaintances was Vala, a Russian émigré who had been a dancer. When my mother decided that I should dance, she asked Vala to suggest a teacher, and I was taken to Olga Preobrazhenskaya (1870–1962). I was lucky;

Preo was one of the most admired teachers of that time. She had been a prima ballerina at Russia's Mariinsky Theater, and she imparted to her students the great tradition of classicism as she had experienced it on the Imperial stages and in the studios of Marius Petipa, Christian Johansson, and Enrico Cecchetti. But her greatest recommendation was that she was a wonderful teacher—clear in her presentation, demanding without being overbearing, and stylistically immaculate.

I think my introduction to dance was fairly typical. Most children begin ballet classes because their parents believe ballet is an activity that will benefit the child. Eventually, the child's interest may surpass that of the parent, and a dancer in the making is born!

In America's early colonial days and through the nineteenth century, French and Italian dancers performed in our major cities. Some were hired to teach dance and deportment (manners) to young ladies of good families. Some settled here and taught privately. But ballet did not flourish in American culture until the beginning of the twentieth century. At this time Russian dancers, such as Anna Pavlova, toured the country and introduced the Russian style to bemused audiences. Additionally, many major cities supported opera houses with resident ballet companies. The Russian Revolution brought the greatest influx of Russian dancers and teachers to these shores.

The Revolution also forced Diaghilev's Ballets Russes to remain in the West. After Diaghilev's death in 1929, the company performed under the names of Ballets Russes de Monte Carlo and Ballets Russes du Colonel de Basil. By that time, most of the original dancers had left the stage and were teaching in Europe and the United States. The style taught today in America owes much to these early émigrés, including Mikhail

Fokine, Adolph Bolm (1884–1951), Michael Mordkin (1880–1944), Piotr Vladimiroff (1893–1970), and Anatole Oboukhoff (1896–1962). When teachers say they are following a Russian method, they usually mean that their studies come from one of these masters' former students.

The conditions of teaching in America were very different from the ones that saw the flowering of the Russian ballet, a system modeled on the French ballet and used to this day. In the Russian system, ten-year-old children are selected for the State school on the basis of their physical attributes. For eight years, they receive academic as well as dance and music education, undergoing a process of selection every year. Those who make it through to the end (typically around 25 out of the 60 chosen each year) are guaranteed work either in the city where they studied or some other location. Even large companies, like the Kirov or the Bolshoi, cannot guarantee a place for all graduating students. Occasionally an outstanding dancer from the provincial cities, like Mikhail Baryshnikov, who began his studies in Riga, is transferred to the most prestigious Kirov.

When the ties with Mother Russia were broken, most émigré dancers began teaching in open studios, meaning that they employed an ungraded system. Classes were generally at an intermediate or advanced level, and anyone could take them. In the 1930s some teachers began to offer a more systematic approach to dance education, notably Catherine Littlefield (1905–1951) in Philadelphia, George Balanchine (under the auspices of Lincoln Kirstein, 1907–1997) in New York's School of American Ballet, and Marie Rambert (1888–1982) and Ninette de Valois in England.

An open studio generally offers classes on a per-class basis. Although their instruction may be excellent, these studios are best suited to advanced and professional dancers, because they cannot follow a developmental curriculum due to their largely transient student body. However, most dancers studying in the early twentieth century were educated in this fashion.

Today, in the major cities, many studios offer ungraded classes throughout the day, and a graded program for children as well as classes for adults in the late afternoon and evening. In smaller towns, where there is no group of professional dancers, studios generally offer classes for children and adults after school hours. Additionally, many established ballet companies have an associated school, such as the New York City Ballet's School of American Ballet, the San Francisco Ballet and School, the Pacific Northwest Ballet School in Seattle, the Houston Ballet and School, the National Ballet School in Toronto, and the Royal Winnipeg Ballet School, to name a few.

SELECTING A SCHOOL

In metropolitan areas the choices of dance schools are numerous, which paradoxically makes the search for a teacher more difficult. Selecting a school should not be a casual matter. Most schools and studios have websites or at least a presence on the Internet. While this is a wonderful way to discover the studio options in your vicinity, website information should only be a starting point for selecting a school. Opting for the convenience of a studio close to home should be weighed against the reputation of the school. Even personal recommendations from other parents are also helpful to investigate.

A visit to the school and a talk with the teacher are wise, once you have a studio in mind. Observing a few classes (not only the one your child will attend, but also a couple of other levels to ascertain the progress of the students) and making a note of the teacher's relationship to the students and the tone maintained in class will shed light on the kind of experience your child might receive.

This initial effort is important for one overriding reason: when you have chosen a school you must be prepared to make a commitment, because changing schools may be detrimental to the progress of the child. Learning to dance is similar to learning any other skill. It requires consistency and enough time for the skill to be assimilated and to become second nature. Although all ballet teachers presumably teach ballet technique, some stylistic differences are common. For a pirouette (turn), Teacher A may favor a preparation in fourth position with both legs in plié (bent knees), while Teacher B likes the back leg to be straight. A child who takes classes that advocate contrasting styles does not have the chance to assimilate either method, and will not be able to improve the performance of these turns because of the confusing messages transmitted to the muscles.

Types of Dance Schools

PRIVATE STUDIOS

Most dancers begin by taking classes at a private studio. Only when their interest and talent are assured will they seek a professional school or an arts high school to further their studies. Private dance schools or studios can offer a wide variety of programs. They are usually privately owned, and may range in size from one room in a residence to entire buildings comprised of numerous studio spaces.

A studio is usually administered by the principal teacher, who makes all decisions pertaining to its operation, including the hiring of other teachers. Many studios find it necessary for tax purposes to apply for nonprofit status, in which case a board of directors is selected. More often than not, the teacher will retain control by being a board member.

These studios may specialize in ballet and offer tap and jazz classes; an increasing number include modern dance in their curricula. A potential student can determine the emphasis a studio places on any one discipline by looking at its schedule of classes; more classes will be offered in the studio's favored technique.

Even relatively small private studios may have a performing group to provide an artistic outlet for their older students. Additionally, many private studios join organizations, such as the Dance Masters of America or the National Association of Dance Artists, which provide a forum for local teachers and an opportunity for students to take classes with a variety of teachers in ballet, tap, jazz, hip-hop, and modern.

Most schools form their classes by age group and level of proficiency. This grading takes into consideration the physical development of the children and the number of years they have been dancing, and may thus span two or three years. For example, a class may include a nine-year-old who has been dancing for three years and an eleven-year-old who has only one year of experience. Some schools follow a syllabus, like the Vaganova system, the Cecchetti method, or the Royal Academy of Dancing (the method developed in England in the 1930s that formed the basis of British ballet). More often than not the principal teacher or director follows the training method that she or he studied, or with which she or he was professionally associated. For example, a teacher who was a member of the New York City Ballet will probably subscribe to the ideas advanced by George Balanchine and hire teachers who share that approach, thus creating a homogeneous base for all instruction carried out at the school.

Unless the school specifies its affiliation by declaring that it teaches a specific method, it can be assumed that the technique taught is a good old American hybrid. This melting pot is alive and well in the dance field and has produced some outstanding performers as well as pedagogues.

In large cities, some schools operate on the model of the open studio. They offer ungraded classes that students can attend without having to enroll for a full semester. These classes are usually at an intermediate or advanced level, and are therefore beneficial to dancers who have reached a level of proficiency that allows them to take full advantage of the material covered in the class.

DANCE PROGRAMS IN PUBLIC SCHOOLS

In the past thirty or more years the value of arts education has received wider recognition, although it continues to fluctuate. While music, visual arts, and, in some instances, theatre have been an integral part of the education of our children for a long time, dance is a relative newcomer to the scene. In the 1980s, a strong thrust to establish dance education in public schools created dance programs in many states. The number or schools offering dance curriculum has tapered recently, and according to a 2009–2010 report conducted by the US Department of Education (*Arts Education in Public Elementary Schools: 1999–2000 and 2009–2010*), only three percent of elementary schools reported any dance-specific curriculum, a 20 percent decrease from ten years prior. Within these public schools all programs are not equal. Michelle Mathesius, assistant principal at La Guardia High School of Music and the Performing Arts, warned that a distinction must be made between enrichment programs and dance education:

> The dance education I refer to focuses on sequential and highly specialized training leading to a professional career—serious dance education as distinguished from what might be termed "enrichment programs." I have nothing against enrichment programs as long as they make no false promises to those they serve. Unfortunately, many of today's programs fall into the enrichment category while implicitly promising that which can be delivered only through dance education. (*Journal of Physical Education, Recreation and Dance*, February 1992)

Mathesius succinctly outlines the elements that distinguish dance education from an enrichment program.

1. There must be a large pool of candidates from which to recruit . . . There must be a rigorous audition process that all but guarantees the selection of highly motivated and extremely talented young dancers.
2. The faculty must be composed of artist/teachers—those that have dance expertise as a result of their dance performance experience.
3. Technique classes, the nuts and bolts of dance education, should be held sacred. Technical mastery is an essential goal and must be carefully taught with a regimen of daily classes in classical ballet and modern dance.

4. Live music is a vital component of every dance class. Any serious institute which trains dancers for the profession, without exception, provides each technique class with a musician.

5. A syllabus must be followed for technique classes that reflects demanding requirements and standards at all levels.

A number of states offer dance as part of arts education beyond enrichment through their magnet programs (see appendix for listings). While the majority of these schools are high schools, a few elementary schools also specialize in the arts. When exploring these school options, be sure to consider the individual school's definition of "enrichment program."

Typically, dance programs at magnet schools follow the model of a conservatory and are staffed by teachers who were professional dancers. Two to three hours of the school day are devoted to dance, a schedule that allows at least one technique class a day. The programs accept students through an audition process and offer ballet, modern dance, jazz, and sometimes tap. They may offer additional classes in dance history, kinesiology, or composition. Some, like New World School of the Arts in Miami, Florida, have classes in cultural dance.

Some school districts have Artist-in-Residence programs, through which an individual or a company may spend from one week to a full year at the school, working with the students. In a few instances, through the efforts of individual teachers, a dance program has grown from an extracurricular activity to a recognized entity within the broader curriculum of the school.

The early years of training are critical in a dancer's career; children who show both interest and promise need a program with the technical training that will allow them to fulfill their potential.

PRIVATE HIGH SCHOOLS

A number of private schools in the United States specialize in arts education and include a dance focus: the Interlochen Arts Academy in Michigan; the Walnut Hill School for the Arts in Massachusetts; the Professional Children's School in New York; the Idyllwild School of Music and the Arts and the Crossroads School, both in California; and the Chicago Academy for the Arts. These schools offer a comprehensive arts and academic education (although the Crossroads School does not offer dance among its specialized majors). The students specialize in their chosen art form, but admission is generally granted through an audition process that tests both academic and artistic skills.

The advantages of attending these schools are numerous. They combine the benefits of a high school, where students receive their general education, with a studio program in the arts that is otherwise only available through a private studio. These schools typically offer a broad spectrum of dance technique classes taught by professionals, and supplementary subjects generally not taught in private studios, such as dance history, kinesiology, and composition; and of course they provide performing experience. They prepare the students for professional careers and for furthering their arts educations in university programs.

But perhaps the greatest contribution of these schools is the environment they provide, in which the students can grow as artists among kindred souls, within a community that appreciates and caters to this special group. There is no need to sacrifice social life, which is too often the price paid by dancers who attend dance classes after school.

For many dancers, a private high school for the arts offers a solution to the problem of obtaining a broad education without compromise.

PROFESSIONAL SCHOOLS

Usually a child is placed in a professional school after several years of preliminary training. Some professional schools, however, offer programs for young, beginning students. For older students, entrance into a professional school is generally by audition.

Some schools have a two-track program: the more serious students interested in a dance career follow one track, while the students who are attending mainly for recreation follow another. The Hartford School of Ballet in Hartford, Connecticut, is one school that offers this kind of program. Some schools will not accept students with previous training older than fourteen (the School of American Ballet) or sixteen (the Joffrey School). However, their summer schools accept older students. These schools routinely recruit talented students and are sometimes able to offer substantial scholarships.

Professional schools, because of their affiliation with companies, generally subscribe to a particular style and employ teachers who have been trained in that style: Vaganova's style (Russian) at the Hartford Ballet's school; the Italian style at the New York Theatre Ballet School; Balanchine's style at the School of American Ballet.

One of the many advantages of attending a professional school is the opportunity to take part in the productions of the sister company, such as the annual *Nutcracker*. Unlike the performances presented by private studios, where the students are the main performers, these productions place children within a greater whole. They allow them to learn the manners of the stage by watching professionals, who exemplify the standards toward which the children strive.

However, the competition at these schools is often fierce, and the demands for a high standard unbending. At times the individual personalities and needs of the students become secondary to their technical achievements; and while the students develop their technical skills, other aspects of their growth may be overlooked. Suzanne Gordon, in her book *Off Balance: The Real World of Ballet* (1983), writes about the overwhelming schedule at the School of American Ballet, which can still ring true in some professional schools:

> Student dancers, like professionals, study six days a week. As they advance, they must do schoolwork, as well as take two or three classes a day. At the most advanced levels, they often dance in company productions; added to their normal course work are rehearsals and performances. This leaves little time for socializing . . . In the world of ballet, dancers are often discouraged from engaging in any activity that might draw their attention away from dance.

While the top professional schools are the training ground for some outstanding performers, an all-or-nothing attitude instilled in their students can preclude an objective assessment of the options open to dancers.

The lure of New York and San Francisco is very strong for many dancers intent on a career; they perceive these two coastal cities as the apex of the profession. Yet the level of instruction in America today offers alternatives without compromise. Many dancers in New York received their initial training elsewhere; their competence attests to the standards set by their hometown schools and cannot be underestimated. Additionally, most major cities are graced today by a ballet company. Annual audition listings and the jobs guide compiled by *Dance* Magazine demonstrate the extensive choices dancers have for a fulfilling professional career.

Caution: The Internet and Technology

As much as technology can be a helpful tool to aid in discovering what is available, when learning to dance, the Internet is not a credible place for how-to information. The only place for a young dancer to learn the art form is in the studio with a live teacher and other students in the room. Hands-on correction, instant feedback, and attention to detail take place during a face-to-face instructional experience. Sharing movement and energy with others in a studio is an integral part of dance training, so beware of Internet courses that claim to teach ballet online or offer ballet classes remotely via two-dimensional media. A quick search might reveal one such course, which lures you to "become a professional ballet dancer," and offers an online experience called, *Learn Ballet on the Fly!* There are YouTube videos that claim you can "teach yourself ballet." These ridiculous offerings are not worth your time or money. One does not learn ballet "on the fly." Mastering the art form demands years of dedication and rigorous training. Even perfecting the motions on a beginning level needs the careful scrutiny of a teacher who can correct posture and placement. The study of ballet is not intended for the privacy of your own home. A studio atmosphere provides the necessary space and community, and a teacher evaluates musicality, and full body alignment. Ballet is a physical form with details meant to be attended to by an outside eye, not absorbed alone or studied passively.

Technology can be useful in some ways, however. If a young dancer is interested in peripheral studies, such as the history of ballet or pedagogy, there are valid opportunities to study such material online and the offerings are constantly changing and expanding. It is not always necessary to be at the college level for participation in such courses. Some valuable supplemental information can be found via technology with careful screening and a bit of education in advance.

Likewise, viewing film, video, and television can have a great impact on a young dancer's perception of training. Hollywood and TV have tended to glorify and over-dramatize the field of ballet by stressing negative aspects of training—such as fierce competition and dysfunctional angry artistic directors—for the sake of drama and storytelling. Technique may be portrayed as easy or unachievable or any number of other extremes. It's wise to remember that this is generally fiction. Even "reality" television is created to highlight the dramatic, rather than depict actual reality. Some documentaries present a more realistic perspective, albeit one selected by television or Hollywood producers. Several documentaries are quite well done and can highly influence a young dancer's perception of what is possible, and what the business and training of dance is all about. Public television can be a generally reliable source for dance documentaries and recorded performances.

The countless videos found floating around on the Internet can either be discouraging, or a source of inspiration. Seeking out footage of a professional ballet company performance may demonstrate to youngsters the value of technique, and in some cases bring the concept of performance to those who do not generally have access to attending a live concert. But viewing YouTube or other online channels should always be considered supplementary to a dancer's studio education. After all, there are no guidelines or standards to what is posted online, so the legitimacy and accuracy of the information will always remain in question.

ABOUT TEACHERS

Thanks to college programs in dance, dancers today are as likely as other professionals to have a degree, yet there are still many dance teachers who bypassed this qualification because of their professional commitments.

Modern dancers are more likely than ballet dancers to have a college degree. They often start dancing at a later age, and tend to be more cerebral in their approaches to dance. This allows them to weigh teaching methods and to be more impartial in their approach.

In contrast, the traditional path for a ballet dancer takes the student from a preprofessional school through the ranks of the corps de ballet, to a position as a soloist in a company. However, in today's competitive world dancers realize the need for formal education, and many pursue degrees and a professional career at the same time. After a professional performing career, the dancer sometimes turns to teaching. Former dancers who seek a postperformance career college degree are the latest wave of what universities dub "returning professionals." It goes without saying that dance teachers have, at the very least, been through rigorous and formal dance training themselves.

Throughout the thirty-odd years that encompass the training period and the professional career, a dancer may study with a variety of teachers in different schools and join various companies, as the need to work with a certain choreographer or a particular repertoire dictates. The better qualified, more adaptable dancer will find greater opportunities.

Dancers are gypsies. They go where work is available, stay as long as they are challenged and appreciated, and move on, either because they have been offered better contracts or because their present contracts have not been renewed. Eventually they may return to their hometowns and open up schools. Many adopt new cities and teach at the school of the company in which they perform.

Economic realities play a large role in determining when a dancer begins to teach. Many dancers are freelance artists, dancing with one group and then with another, often with periods of no engagements in between; to supplement their incomes, they may teach. However, schools that rely on professionally active dancers to make up their faculty may inadvertently do a disservice to their student body by failing to provide continuity in the training. This consideration is especially true for the beginning levels, when consistency is very important.

At the turn of the century, renowned ballet master Enrico Cecchetti wrote an open letter to his students in Russia cautioning them to choose teachers who had completed their performing careers. The reason for this injunction is still valid today: dancers are in training throughout their performing careers, necessarily focusing on personal solutions to the challenges of their technique. After they have stopped dancing, dancers may find the leisure to reflect on the technique as a whole and to begin to recognize how it affects body types that are different from their own.

Language gives us a further clue to the transition that every dancer must make to become a teacher—we say a dancer "takes" class, whereas a teacher "gives" class. Thus teachers refocus their attention to become fully responsive to the needs of their students. In guiding them through the technique, teachers offer their knowledge as a gift to their students, who take the gift and further fashion it to meet their individual requirements. A teacher who is concerned about his or her own execution of the movement, rather than that of the students, generally indicates one who is not yet ready to "give" a class. Some people make the transition from dancer to teacher more gracefully than others, and they are the ones who make the better teachers. Furthermore, the level of proficiency or recognition a teacher achieved during his or her career does not guarantee greater effectiveness as a teacher. A prima ballerina is not necessarily a better teacher than someone who has only been in the corps de ballet.

The teacher you select will probably have a list of professional credentials that establish her or his lineage and competence and indicate the type of technique to be taught. She or he may also have a college degree in dance or be certified to teach through a specific technical training such as the Royal Academy of Dance (RAD), or by the state, if employed in the public school system. A parent should feel free to ask for teachers' credentials and discuss with teachers the focus or approach that guides them. Coupled with observation of a class or two, interviews will provide a basis for determining good style and making a selection. The school website should provide preliminary information, but asking for details will still be necessary.

Children initially learn by imitating their teachers, so it is important that teachers exhibit a clean body line free of mannerisms. All dancers develop idiosyncrasies—individual ways of performing motions that, when they do not interfere with the clarity of the gesture, can enhance and deepen expressiveness. However, when dancers become teachers, they must shed these mannerisms in order to transmit a pure line to their students. The ways teachers hold themselves, demonstrate the movements, and offer correction give testimony to the training they received; as with antiques, provenance is of utmost importance. Teachers should be able to explain the meanings of the French names used in the class and to fully engage the attention of their pupils. (To some extent the French terminology is used by all techniques, so this knowledge will help the young dancer in training within any Western dance form.)

Some teachers routinely attend summer workshops. These typically one- to two-week sessions are good forums for exchanging ideas as well as honing skills (particularly for young teachers), but they cannot replace a good early education and professional experience in the field. It takes years to integrate a technique, and while new concepts learned at summer workshops can serve to clarify teachers' ideas, they should not be used as a claim that the teacher is proficient in the method.

The ideal teacher should possess the following:

1. Credentials from a recognized institution: a professional school, company, or college
2. Some professional experience
3. A patient but not pampering attitude
4. Comfort with the material, and an ability to organize the material logically and appropriately for each age group

5. An ability to inspire a feeling of purpose and excitement among the students
6. A critical eye for making appropriate criticism in an encouraging manner
7. An ability to maintain concentration and discipline at all times
8. Above all, a love for the experience of dance, and an unselfish desire to see the students improve.

The Teacher's Role

The interaction between teacher and student is probably one of the most important aspects of the learning process; teachers must not only be knowledgeable, but must also possess a generosity of spirit that enables them to share their knowledge.

Dancers often suffer from low self-esteem. We tend to be overly critical and demanding of our performance and to accept compliments with strong reservations. Teachers who establish their authority through fear and humiliation can feed this insecurity and damage both the individual and the dance. Although maintaining discipline in the studio is essential to good learning, other methods are available besides intimidation. By engaging the interest of the student, the teacher can diminish the need to enforce silence. Within a couple of years of study students realize that they do not want to be distracted, that they need to direct all of their concentration toward the execution of the movement, and they derive pleasure from mastering the task.

In addition to the overtly physical training that takes place in class, another type of learning is taking place. Class time can serve as a time of meditation. We can retire from the everyday world to concentrate deeply on our own ability, looking toward the strength within that is the source of discipline. We admire artists for their ability to give themselves to the moment of creation, and we are told that in each of us there is an artist crying to be heard. Dance class provides that access; the teacher, like the Zen master, sets the tone and the example and leads students on a journey of self-discovery.

STRUCTURE OF STUDIES

A good school will provide continuity in instruction; in other words, it will have scheduled, progressive, or graded classes conducted by the same teacher throughout the year. Students need to become familiar with a teacher's style of presentation and pace. Only then can they begin to concentrate on the concepts that are presented, and only then can their progress be gauged. Any one lesson will be entirely devoted to a specific discipline, either ballet, tap, modern, or jazz. Your child will be placed at the appropriate level, and the teacher will suggest additional classes for the student to attend as she or he progresses through the curriculum. In the case of beginners who only take one class a week, a full hour is absolutely necessary in order to instill the principles of technique. After the student begins to take two or more classes a week, the necessity for the full class time to be devoted to one discipline is even more important. By that time, the student will know more vocabulary and will need to practice it. Class time should normally increase to an hour and a quarter and then an hour and a half, which is the traditional length of a lesson. Once pointe work is introduced, the class may stretch to two hours.

We know that online courses and videos cannot replace the live experience of a teacher and student working face-to-face in a studio. Yet there are benefits to other technological tools, such as video cameras and personal electronic devices. Easily accessible now, any number of devices can be used to aid a student's progress in the studio. For example, a teacher might record a class exercise on video and instantly allow the students to watch the footage of themselves for feedback, recognition of bad habits, or correct execution. Or a teacher may also choose to photograph a student in effort to help them literally see what they are doing. Some studios host online forums providing a place for dancers to share information about anything from technique levels and class progress to the types of shoes they like best. These teaching tools may or may not surface within a particular style of instruction, and may occasionally add outside "homework" for the serious dance student.

THE TALENTED CHILD

The talented child will always attract attention and receive special encouragement from instructors. Beware, however, of the teacher or studio director who inappropriately pushes the child through the curriculum too quickly. Children with greater natural facility will execute the technique easily and with more accuracy than those less gifted. They may give the impression that they are ready, both emotionally and physically, to go on to the next level. Young musculature, however, requires time to develop to support the dance movements fully. Skipping through levels will leave big gaps in a child's integration and understanding of the technique and may ultimately result in areas of physical stress that are very difficult to correct. Hurrying the process is both unwise and unnecessary. If the musculature is not adequately prepared, the child will strain to achieve the positions demanded and will develop bad habits, such as areas of compensation—using the wrong muscles to produce a motion. In the end, the young dancer will have built an unresponsive musculature that may well overshadow natural talent.

The parent of the talented child needs to be alert to the motivation of teachers who push a child too fast. Are these teachers promoting the best interest of the child, or their own reputations? Ultimately, only the talent of the dancer is needed for promotion. The most brilliant teacher cannot make a dancer from an unwilling or unsuitable body or soul. In fact, teachers do not "make" dancers at all; a good teacher will lead the student through an ever-deeper understanding of the technique to the realization of her or his potential. The credit belongs to the student. Teachers may take pride that they have given the correct information, and may rejoice in the achievements of their pupils. In summary, the type of school you select will depend upon the age and the needs of your child. Even if your public school offers a dance program, you may want to enroll your child in a private studio program for a more concentrated training. If your initial choice of a school was a good one, there should be no need to switch. A serious studio will usually offer a program that leads students from the beginning to a preprofessional level. You may, however, want to consider enrolling your child in a private arts high school if she or he demonstrates a keen interest and shows promise.

Even the smallest cities offer some choice of instruction. In larger cities the school associated with a ballet company may provide more intense instruction; however, independent studios can be equally demanding and of high quality. In all cases, go beyond the Internet to obtain detailed information about your options.

Even if you are quite sure that your child has no intention of becoming a professional dancer and is simply looking for a good activity, it is advisable to choose a reputable school for early training. If children study at a school that honors the traditional principles of ballet technique they will experience something real, something of lasting value that will give them a deep appreciation of the art form and will enrich their lives forever. Similarly, if you are lucky enough to live in an area that offers creative and modern dance for children, the experience of the discovery of movement, the ability to develop self-expression, and the broadening of the base of spatial perceptions will enhance your child's intellectual, physical, and emotional growth.

As the student grows and gains a basic grasp of the fundamental motions, she or he is ready to learn more of the specific steps and patterns of the ballet technique. Students from the School of Madison Ballet, Madison, Wisconsin. © 2015 Maureen Janson

4

PROGRESSION OF TRAINING

THE TENDENCY TO PROGRAM A child's day with a variety of
activities leaves little time for leisure and play. Admittedly, parents struggle with balancing careers and family and generally
want to make sure that their children are engaged in worthwhile activities. I once received an inquiry about dance classes
for a five-year-old. When I told the mother that this preballet
class met on Tuesdays, she answered, "I will have to see if I can
reschedule my daughter's tennis lesson." The task of resched-
uling was daunting because the child also studied piano, took
swimming lessons, and participated in an acting workshop.

This overscheduling coupled with increasingly short
attention spans fueled by the instancy of electronic communication has a side effect. People tend to become dabblers
who invest a minimum of effort in their work, want the maximum return, and, when gratification is not instant, move on
to the next thing. As we spend more and more time texting
and expecting instant answers, results, or communication,
already busy days begin to feel jam-packed.

Something has also been lost in this process of filling
the day with named endeavors and electronic correspon-
dence. The happiest memories from my childhood all stem
from the hours I spent either alone or with friends playing
unstructured games, inventing stories to act out or dance,

building ships out of chairs, dressing in my mother's clothes, or, because it was a safer world then, taking the long way home from school to explore different parts of the city. Now we have television, video games, or the Internet to interfere with our creative urges, shape our perceptions, and keep us rooted as spectators instead of participants.

In dance, as in other art forms, or indeed in any activity, a sincere commitment to the task is the first necessity. Learning to dance is a long-term commitment, because the rewards are not immediately evident. It is essential for parents to appreciate this process.

Every year, a number of new students at any particular school decide that they do not like to dance after a couple of lessons. More often than not, the parents tell the teacher about the problem before allowing the child to give up. In some cases tuition is not refundable, so many parents continue to bring the child to class for the remainder of the semester. The majority of these children who stay on begin to enjoy class after a few more weeks of practice and insist on continuing after the first semester is over.

Learning to enjoy the process is an integral part of learning to dance. The process consists of little steps, small triumphs, small challenges, and some disappointments that may lead to new understanding. Each level of ballet includes movements that illustrate a particular usage of the body and develop the musculature while enlarging the student's range and vocabulary of motion. Students' progress is not based on the number of new steps learned but rather on the gradual improvement in execution. It takes a long time to become a dancer—sometimes up to ten years before a solid intermediate level is reached. Thus, it is important to honor the process and praise the child at each level of development.

DEVELOPING GOOD POSTURE

Certain features of ballet technique are stressed from the beginning of training and continue to be perfected throughout a dancer's life. Foremost among these features is good posture. When considering that ballet training engages the body symmetrically through exercises that train one side of the body at a time, this task involves the awareness that the supporting side is active, although it does not move. The primary goal of early training is to achieve a balanced and aligned stance. Standing correctly aligned on two legs with the ability to transfer your body weight to one leg without losing this alignment are prerequisites for all motion. Thus the pelvis does not move when a leg is lifted off the floor. (In initial training, the legs do not rise above 45 degrees; later in training, with higher extension, the pelvis participates in the motion.) The shoulder does not rise when an arm is lifted into position. This ability is developed through the execution of a few exercises that foster strength in all the weight-bearing joints (hip, knee, ankle) as well as engage the muscles of the torso to strengthen the spine. Of course, all motions are performed with a degree of turnout and with the arms held in a rounded manner.

The ability to maintain a balanced stance depends upon the child's physical development. The development of the musculature proceeds at its own pace; some children are naturally more coordinated and kinetically aware than others and can thus reproduce the movement they see with more accuracy. Starting ballet classes before age seven will not necessarily produce a prodigy. It instead tends to prolong this initial stage of training and often results in the child deciding to stop lessons just at the time when she or he would be moving into a more exciting phase.

Correct posture is achieved through the practice of the basic vocabulary. These steps are the building blocks of all future motions; within them they encompass all the permutations of the ballet technique. As mentioned earlier, these simple exercises create new synaptic connections that will allow the body to respond immediately to commands from the brain. In his seminal work on child development, Jean Piaget (1896–1980) identified the period from birth to age seven as the preoperational stage. At this stage, thought and action have not yet developed the relationship that as adults we take for granted: we can externalize (manifest) our thought directly into action. Young children will often have trouble guiding their actions, because they have not yet developed a direct link between thought and action. This inability, along with a short attention span, severely curtails the kinds of physical activities that children can successfully participate in before age seven. The first two or three years of dance training are as basic to the development of the ballet technique as learning to crawl is to the child, and they carry the same implications: the motions learned become part of the innate vocabulary.

There was a woman who lived down the street from me in London who had a congenital hip defect that made her walk with a pronounced limp. Her three children also walked with a limp, even though they had not inherited the hip defect; they had simply learned to walk by imitating their mother.

Once the body is "placed" and the student has a basic grasp of the fundamental motions, she or he is ready to learn more of the steps of the technique, and class becomes more varied. There are only about 56 steps in the classical technique, but the ways in which they can be combined are endless.

Progression through the technique consists of improving the execution of the motions as well as building stamina. It is not until a high-intermediate level has been reached that certain steps of the technique can be practiced; therefore, the vocabulary of motions is quite limited for the first six or seven years of training. The stretch of the instep, the line of the leg, the fluidity of the arms, secure balance, and smoothness of transitions are some of the markers that indicate progress in integrating the technique. These elements remain the primary concern of dancers throughout their life.

POINTE WORK

Most young dancers dream of dancing on pointe. It is perhaps the closest one can be to human flight, yet still be connected to the ground. The mental image of a professional ballet dancer usually is of a dancer on pointe, appearing otherwordly in a long romantic tutu, perhaps slowly turning on a music box while balanced on one leg.

The road to rising on pointe is not always so dreamy. Generally, after about four years of serious study, the student is ready to begin pointe work. The classroom preparation for this full rise onto the toes consists of exercises performed on half-pointe that strengthen the foot and familiarize the body with balancing on a smaller surface than the whole foot provides. Additionally, through preliminary regular classes, the student will have developed a strong back and a degree of control through the torso and the hip joint that allow maintenance of proper alignment.

It must be emphasized that the technique of dancing on pointe is not different from the technique required to perform the rest of the ballet vocabulary. The strength of the spine, hip, knee, and ankle joints is essential for the execution of all dance movements. Good alignment and a well-developed instep facilitate dancing both on pointe and off pointe. However, the extra effort required to rise on pointe and the ability to maintain a controlled light stance must be well developed before pointe work is introduced.

Uncommon, yet not entirely unusual, is that the male student may also be prompted to study pointe work. Some professional contemporary repertory requires pointe work of male dancers, so an introduction at a younger age may be beneficial and in some cases, encouraged.

Not all feet develop the required curvature for dancing on pointe. Children with insufficiently arched feet will find going on pointe difficult regardless of their proficiency in other areas. Similarly, those with very high arches will have problems because their ankles and insteps will not offer adequate support. In both cases, practice helps both to develop the arch further and stabilize the ankle joint.

Initially, ten to fifteen minutes is sufficient time to practice pointe work after the regular technique class. For the more advanced students, most schools schedule a full class on pointe once or twice a week. However, it will take a couple of years from the time children first go on pointe until they exhibit an adequate knowledge of the vocabulary and are physically able to cope with a full class on pointe.

The question of when to put a child on pointe has always stirred controversy. Some teachers have their students on pointe as early as age nine (which, in my opinion, is too early); others wait until the child is twelve. Establishing a desirable age between these two extremes is difficult because so much depends on the child's physical development and her ability to maintain the correct alignment. But to err on the side of conservatism is better. The bones of the foot are among the last to ossify; in other words, they remain relatively soft until the late teens. The arch of the foot, with training, can continue to increase until the bones have fully matured. Going on pointe too early can disrupt this process and permanently injure the foot.

Also, the child must be taking at least three classes a week before pointe is added to his or her schedule. With the addition, initially, of one full class on pointe, these four classes will ensure a correct progression and maintenance of the technique. However, a half hour of pointe after the technique class serves as well as a separately scheduled pointe class.

For the student who simply enjoys dance, without thoughts of becoming a professional, three classes a week are sufficient. The career-track student will eventually take a daily ballet class wearing old pointe shoes (too soft for pointe work) instead of regular soft slippers, and will probably do part of each class on pointe.

TRAINING BOYS

In the preparatory stages, the technique for boys and girls is the same. In most professional schools boys and girls attend different classes, with female teachers teaching girls and male teachers teaching boys. Unfortunately, in most studios there are not enough boys enrolled to warrant a separate class. However, boys may initially attend classes for reasons other than learning to dance—the dance studio is a great place to meet girls. One studio that had a substantial male enrollment decided to form a special class for the boys, only to see them give up dancing because the reason for their attendance was taken away.

W. Earle Smith, artistic director of the Madison Ballet company in Wisconsin, which offers an affiliated training school, has found the opposite in his boys/mens class. He says he first began teaching the class as an effort to "give young boys an opportunity to share a passion with other young boys." Smith felt that initially many young men and boys shied away from dance classes because they felt alone. Teaching a group between the ages of nine and 13, he has found success with the class for nearly 20 years.

At the intermediate level boys need to develop specific technical skills, and a class geared to their requirements is beneficial. Male dancers need training that will not only develop a high jump, but also give them the strength to lift a partner. A class for male dancers is therefore typically designed to emphasize strength-building. There are also some marked differences in the execution of turns; often the male dancer does not rise on pointe, so he performs a windup action as the turn begins. This type of action is not part of the female dancer's training.

Additionally, the masculine style of presentation—how the dancer holds himself, how he walks or stands—is very different from the feminine style. If a male teacher is not available for a boys' class at a school, the female teacher must be aware of these differences and make sure that the boys in her class develop the correct style. Attending dance performances and watching ballet performance videos will provide some additional guidance to the young boy. Much of the young dancer's training relies on osmosis, so seeing the right role models will prompt him to imitate the correct style.

Boys may be expected to perform movements for which their musculature has not been adequately prepared and that may be physically harmful. Just as dancers should not be put on pointe too early, they must not be allowed to lift their partners before their back and leg muscles are up to the task. (Again it is hard to provide a specific age because physiques differ so widely; a fourteen-year-old with a strong musculature may be able to perform some lifts and partnering that an eighteen-year-old with a frail physique cannot engage in safely.)

Although schools give scholarships more readily to boys than to girls, the more talented are still all too easily lured by the more prestigious schools. As with girls, parents should guard against the exploitive aspects of the dance world and consider their child's emotional and physical welfare, especially when scholarship offers include the need to send the child away from home.

However, boys can typically start dancing at a later age than girls and still excel in ballet, modern dance, and jazz. Many male modern dancers do not discover dance until their college years. Rudolf Nureyev (1938–1993) is the most stellar example of a ballet dancer who started training when he was seventeen.

CROSS-TRAINING

We know it is not out of the question, although not traditional, for a young male dancer to learn pointe work. Likewise, contemporary trends in ballet choreography may demand that a female student lift or support a partner. The more advanced female dancer is wise to seek training outside of the ballet realm to acquire the upper body strength necessary for lifting. As choreographic styles and demands expand, to supplement technical training, most dancers who move beyond the intermediate level seek conditioning and cross-training methods.

Studying modern dance, tap, and jazz dance will broaden the student's stylistic understanding. Undertaking a regimen of other activities, such as swimming or Pilates, allows a rounding out of the physical potential of dance training. Since ballet is not necessarily aerobic (some lengthy jumping combinations do demand strong lungs), swimming assists with building stamina. Pilates exercises focus on maintaining a strong and controlled torso. Many dancers use yoga training as a supplement to their technique classes, in order to increase flexibility and challenge balance. Gentle weight-lifting may help dancers, particularly those who are learning to lift, but it is not recommended for all dancers, as it creates an undesirable tightness and bulk.

Cross-training can help the dancers avoid injury as well as recover from it. Dancers need to find methods that help keep the body strong but supple, and the right balance will vary depending on the dancer. For example, one who is hypermobile need not focus on stretching by way of a yoga class, whereas a Pilates class could aid the dancer in stabilizing the overflexible joints.

Former modern dancer Eric Franklin experimented with elastic bands and various sizes of rubber balls in effort to increase his own flexibility, build his strength, release tension, and better his balance. Eventually he designed an exercise regimen geared specifically toward the needs of dancers. In his book *Conditioning for Dance: Training for Peak Performance in All Dance Forms* (2004), Franklin uses ballet terminology and vocabulary to describe a series of practical exercises and conditioning routines. Because this popular cross-training method targets dancers directly, many incorporate Franklin's routines independently into their training schedule.

JUDGING A YOUNG DANCER'S POTENTIAL

It is not surprising that parents should want to know if their child has the ability and talent to pursue a career in dance if the life of the family is affected at every turn by the demands of the studio. The daily ballet class is augmented by other types of lessons like pointe or jazz, as well as modern dance and tap. Rehearsal for performances can consume a tremendous amount of time. Most large studios mount an annual production of *The Nutcracker* and, of course, the end-of-the-year recital requires lengthy preparations. With all of these activities, not only the child's but the whole family's life seems to revolve around the dance studio.

Probably more than in any other art form, success in dance is dependent upon the physical makeup of the individual. The right physique, at the very least, provides the vehicle for all other necessary qualities. The ability to see a movement or position and transpose it accurately onto your body is very important and is the first step in kinesthetic awareness. Musicality is another necessary quality, aided by some training in music (classes in singing, solfège, or piano) to help train the ear. But above all, there must be a desire to dance. Many dancers with less-than-perfect instruments grace our stages. Famous Russian teacher Olga

Preobrazhenskaya was regularly thrown out of Marius Petipa's class, in part because she was short and had rounded shoulders. She persevered, and became one of the leading ballerinas of her era.

Parents should not expect the dance teacher to be a soothsayer and predict the student's future. Being in the right place at the right time also figures in the development of a successful career. Clear, unquestionable talent is very rare, and often works against the student unless it is accompanied by an equally clear will to become a dancer. In other words, a child with great physical facility will often not work as hard as a less well endowed one and, as a result, will not develop the necessary strength or precision.

The progression in the acquisition of technique is a steady and measured one, with each consecutive year of study supplying specific information that is built upon in the following year. This yearly progression prepares the musculature and develops motor control as the child grows, allowing for the gradual learning of necessary skills and a refinement in the execution of all technical aspects.

We must distinguish between learning a trick and learning a technique. Tricks are shortcuts that apply to a particular situation; they do not enlarge our knowledge of the technique, nor do they transfer to other areas of learning. Technique, on the other hand, is a cumulative process in which each step leads logically to the next, and the expertise learned in one area relates to all other areas of the activity.

Although we are discussing ballet training, even those children who are clearly on the ballet track should supplement their knowledge of dance with classes in modern dance. This broadens the students' vocabulary base, making the students better dancers.

SUMMER WORKSHOPS

When a child is old enough and proficient enough to benefit from continuing studies during the summer months (generally around age 12), she or he has several options. The teacher may recommend a workshop at a preprofessional school, or, if your dance school remains open, that your child continue to attend classes there. Many summer programs around the country provide excellent instruction and an opportunity for dancers to experience a new teaching approach. Your choice of program will be guided by your teacher's recommendation, which in turn depends on her or his affiliation. A school that favors the Balanchine style may suggest New York's School of American Ballet, while a Russian-method school will lean toward the Kirov Academy of Ballet in Washington, DC.

There is one unquestionable advantage to attending summer workshops: the opportunity for children to meet and dance with students from different parts of the country, and thus to gauge their levels of proficiency by national standards. However, a number of questions should be asked before you decide to send your child to a summer program. Is the child emotionally mature enough to fully enjoy and benefit from the experience? Is her level of proficiency high enough to enable her to take full advantage of the session? Is the program's method sufficiently in harmony with the current instruction, so that the student's understanding of the technique will be enhanced?

This last question is of particular importance. If the summer program has a different technical basis than the home school, the two teachers will obviously be working against each other to the student's detriment. If the method of instruction is very different from what the student knows, the student will not have the opportunity to test and fully integrate the newfound knowledge.

Additionally, students may sustain injuries from working in a style very different from that of the home school. For example, if the summer faculty stresses a perfect 180-degree turnout while the home school is not as emphatic about it, the student may put too much pressure on the knee and ankle joints in straining to achieve the newly demanded position. Or, if the height of the leg in extensions is emphasized, students may sacrifice their alignment in striving to reach the desired height. For all of these concerns, the home teacher is the best source of information. The teacher knows your child's strengths and weaknesses and can direct her or him to a program that is both conducted at the right level of proficiency and philosophically compatible with the home school's method.

Your child's emotional maturity is also very important. In professional schools an enormous emphasis can be placed on the right physique and weight, especially for girls. Comparing herself to other students in the class, the child may become dissatisfied and feel rejected because she is not getting the attention that thinner girls command. This may lead her to adopt an unreasonable diet regimen that is detrimental to both her physical health and her psyche. (We will speak in more detail on this subject in chapter 9.) A young dancer faces rejection, real or imagined, almost daily: the teacher did not correct her as much as other classmates; others received more accolades; she was not chosen for a part in a production. It is important to choose a program that builds students' self-confidence in a loving environment.

And finally, is the child physically prepared to cope with the rigorous schedule of the summer workshop? If the student has been taking class three times a week, how will her or his body respond to four classes a day?

Besides the professional summer workshops in dance only, numerous summer camps throughout the country emphasize the arts. These offer a worthwhile alternative for children under fourteen who enjoy dancing but are not necessarily planning to become dancers. In these programs, besides dance classes, the children can enjoy art lessons, swimming, and nature walks as well as other athletic and nonathletic activities. The pressure to excel in dance is generally lessened, and the experience can be very positive.

Of course, no single formula is going to address the needs of all dance students. Ideally, a child begins serious dance studies at the age of seven or eight with one class a week. Some schools will expect the second-year student to attend two classes weekly, with the commitment growing to a daily class by age twelve or thirteen. For the recreational student, fewer classes may be adequate. All students over the age of twelve may add other techniques to their curricula; thus pointe, modern dance, jazz, character, and partnering incrementally supplement the ballet class.

It must be remembered that improving technique and keeping the body primed require practice. This can only be achieved in class. Professional dancers rely on a teacher to lead them through a class. Therefore, progression through a dance curriculum demands regular attendance at the scheduled classes.

Dress code varies among schools, but it is standard for students beyond the beginning level to wear black leotards, pink tights, and pink shoes, with hair secured away from the neck for clear postural viewing and unrestricted movement. Students from the School of Madison Ballet, Madison, Wisconsin. © 2015 Maureen Janson

5

WHAT TO WEAR

DANCEWEAR HAS MADE ITS WAY into everyday fashion, and it's hard to remember a world before this was the case. Basic classroom dancewear generally consists of a leotard and tights made of nonrestrictive stretch fabric, from Lycra to cotton, that conforms to the body and allows comfort and ease of movement. But such congenial dress did not always exist.

In the nineteenth century a costumier at the Paris Opera, Monsieur Maillot, invented tights and gave his name to his invention. However, maillots were expensive, as well as bulky (if made of cotton) or fragile (if made of silk). Until the latter part of the nineteenth century female dancers wore tutus in class, and male dancers wore pants and shirts. Teachers taught in street clothes. Cecchetti, the Italian teacher, derided female teachers because they could not demonstrate the movements, encumbered as they were by their long skirts and petticoats. Most female teachers of the late nineteenth and early twentieth centuries taught sitting in a chair. As late as the 1940s Madame Rosanne, a very popular teacher at the studio Wacker in Paris, conducted class from an armchair. As dancing became more athletic, the need for special practice clothes became obvious; but before the explosion in the manufacturing of exercise and workout clothes, dancers dressed in homemade tunics and knitted tights. On stage, they wore silk stockings. These were extra long, designed to reach above the top of the leg and be hidden under the tutu. They were secured by placing several coins under and around the top periphery of the stockings, tying the coins with strings, and then gathering and tying the strings around the waist. This engineering feat produced a smooth-looking leg but was extremely uncomfortable, because the strings cut into the flesh with every motion.

The leotard was also invented in the nineteenth century, by acrobat Jules Leotard. The prototype of this garment covered the upper thighs—not unlike the early version of the male swimsuits—and, unless expertly fitted, tended to bunch up. It was first worn by men because it was traditionally more acceptable for men than for women to reveal their legs; men's ballet costumes of this period often utilized modified versions of the leotard, while women still appeared only in tutus that descended to the knee.

A lot of lore surrounds the use of the layered, warm clothing so dear to dancers. One of the functions of layering, dancers will tell you, is to induce weight loss; the fact that water loss through sweating does not result in real weight loss is somehow glossed over and ignored. In the never-ending pursuit of thinness, dancers resort to promoting as much sweating as possible. To that end, in the faraway days of my training, we wore plastic pants under our leotards and wrapped our thighs in plastic tablecloths. One of the students cut up her mother's tablecloth for this purpose; it had a pattern of little fish, which could be seen swimming upstream under her pink tights. Today dancers can buy all sorts of specially made wraps for every part of the body, but somehow most dancers still prefer the makeshift article, like an extra sweater tied around the waist.

Another function of the layered look, dancers maintain, is to warm the muscles. However, while legwarmers and heavy sweatshirts may help to hold the warmth generated by the body, they do not actually "oil" the muscles, as Alexandra Danilova (1903–1997) liked to describe the warming process. (The first use of legwarmers is attributed to Danilova. She cut the arms off her sweater and wore them on her legs.) The deep lubrication that happens during exercise can only be generated by the body itself. Synovial fluid, which is stored in cartilage, is released through movement, helping reduce friction between the joints.

Often the layering of clothing is necessitated by circumstances. There are many idle minutes during rehearsals when the dancer loses body heat. If the studio is cold and drafty, the extra clothing helps to keep the heat in and prevents the body from cooling down too quickly.

In a London studio where I took class regularly, the heating consisted of a coal stove that smoked when it was first lit in the morning. Our teacher would open the skylight windows in order to get rid of the smoke, and the heat rose with the smoke. We came dressed in legwarmers, heavy socks over our ballet shoes, sweaters, and sometimes, on particularly cold days, woolen hats and mittens. As class progressed the smoke evaporated, the skylight was shut, the room warmed up, and we shed various articles of clothing until we looked less like bag people and more like dancers.

The final function of layering is disguise. Dancers will swath to hide some real or imagined deficiency, as well as real or imagined extra weight. For example, a dancer with an instep that is underdeveloped will wear heavy socks or legwarmers bunched up over the feet; another who is self-conscious about her posterior will drape a sweatshirt around her waist. The idea is that what you cannot see does not exist. Under these circumstances, a teacher needs X-ray eyes to give accurate corrections.

Dance attire is designed not only to provide as much freedom of motion as possible, but also to allow the teacher a clear view of the body for corrections. Teachers routinely demand the shedding of unnecessary layers. Some dance schools have rigid dress codes that make it possible for the teacher to demand specific attire; but as students get older, this enforcement becomes more and more difficult.

Basically, a female dancer needs only tights, a leotard, and shoes. If the weather is cold, a pair of legwarmers and a sweatshirt will make the student more comfortable. Sports apparel designers have recently created moisture-wicking warmer fabrics and designs, such as those worn by Olympic speed skaters. Some styles of sports attire can be suitable as an extra layer for a winter's day in the dance studio. Boys need a good athletic belt, tights, and a t-shirt. Often young boys are more at ease in sweatpants instead of the all-revealing tights. However, sweatshirts and pants conceal too much of the body and thus hinder the teacher in correcting posture and motions.

Light colors are best because they are more revealing. It is easier to see a muscle under a pair of pink (for girls) or gray (for boys) tights than under a pair of black ones. Schools generally have specific colors for each class level or age. This practice gives homogeneity to the class and eliminates any distraction that a riot of colors would produce. When color is not specified, a solid-colored leotard is best. Leotards with bright patterns or bare midriffs are not suitable.

The leotard must fit well: it must not be so large that it bunches around the waist or hips, but must not be so short that the student is forever yanking at it. Remember that the whole attire is designed to provide the least amount of distraction and the greatest amount of comfort, allowing the student to concentrate fully on the motions.

Wearing jewelry in class is discouraged by most teachers, although little post earrings are usually tolerated. The reason for this prohibition is safety. Should a hand inadvertently smack into another person, a ring, bracelet, or watch can become a pain-inducing weapon. Necklaces or chains bounce around when students are jumping and, again, are a hazard, especially in partnering classes. Generally, it is best to come to class unadorned.

To avoid unnecessary purchases, it is always a good idea to determine what the teacher or school will allow the students to wear. This information can often be found on the studio website. For example, the School of Madison Ballet adheres to the following clothing policies posted on their website:

> No jewelry (except small earrings), leg warmers, or extra clothing of any kind may be worn to class. Holes that appear in leotards or tights should be mended immediately. Long-sleeved leotards (not sweaters) are appropriate in cold weather. All students should dress appropriately when arriving and departing class. Dancewear is not appropriate street attire. Students must wear street clothing over their leotards and/or tights when arriving and departing.

SHOES

Shoes are probably the most important item on the dancer's clothing list. Soft slippers, for both boys and girls, must hug the foot and not be too big, especially if the shoes are made of leather, which stretches with use. Unlike regular shoes, the sole of a dance slipper does not extend all the way to the end of the toes or the heel. If the shoe is of inferior quality, its lining will sometimes bunch up at the seam located right under the metatarsals the area of the foot where the dancer stands on half-pointe. This bunching is not only uncomfortable; it can actually cause alignment problems, because the student will shift his or her weight off that area in order to avoid the pressure. Therefore, when buying shoes, check for a smooth seam between the sole and the lining. Also be sure to have the student try on the shoes wearing tights, or socks of a similar weight, for a perfect fit.

Elastic straps secure soft ballet shoes to the dancer's feet. Although some shoes come with elastics attached, in my experience these elastics are usually sewn over the front part of the instep and thus do not ensure against heel slippage. The correct place can be found by folding the heel of the shoe forward over the insole; the elastic should be sewn at the fold.

There are many different ballet shoes on the market today. Leather slippers last longer than canvas ones. Young children usually outgrow their shoes before any real wear-and-tear occurs, so canvas shoes will suffice for them. Some schools recommend specific brands, especially in pointe shoes. Some schools have instituted a shoe-and-leotard pool for the very young students. Outgrown articles of dance clothing are donated to the school to be passed on to children who need them. This practice somewhat eases the financial burden of keeping the student correctly shod.

POINTE SHOES

The fit of the pointe shoe is of the greatest importance for correct alignment and proper development of the foot. At the age of eleven, the day after I joined the ranks of the Petits Rats (dance students at the Paris Opera School) feeling very grown-up, I went to buy my first pair of pointe shoes. Unfortunately, I did not ask anyone's advice and purchased the most comfortable pair of shoes. The vamp was too low and the fit too loose. The shoe did not provide enough support on pointe, and I was miserable until I was fitted properly some time later. As with soft ballet shoes, there are many brands and styles of pointe shoes, differing in hardness and in the support they provide to the foot. The vamp (the upper part of the shoe), should come well above the toe phalanges (metatarsals), and for beginners the tip should be well squared-off, providing a wide surface on which to balance. Additionally, even shoes of the same size and brand may not be exactly alike; therefore, when trying on shoes, ask the salesperson to bring several pairs. Many dancewear stores are staffed by dancers who will not object to your request, so be sure to try an adequate selection. As with soft slippers, wear the tights that are worn in class or socks of a similar weight when trying on the shoes.

Pointe shoes should fit tightly, not slip easily over the heel. Lambswool or gel toe pads can be a good protection for a beginner's feet. Avoid padding that adds too much bulk inside the shoe. Some prefer the lambswool for its absorbing properties, as pads made of plastic do not breathe. Advanced dancers usually do not wear anything extra in their shoes; at most, a small piece of paper towel covers the toes to prevent slippage. Newspaper is also an excellent cover. And toenails should be clipped short enough so that the tip of the toe, rather than the nail, is the only part of the toe that comes in contact with the shoe when the dancer stands on pointe.

Ribbons secure pointe shoes to the dancer's feet. Generally the ribbons are not made preattached to the shoe and are a separate purchase. As soon as possible, sewing the ribbons should become the responsibility of the dancer. Sewing the ribbons by machine is fine, although it only takes minutes to sew them by hand. On occasion, some dancers choose to darn the tips of pointe shoes; not only does the darning with thick cotton provide extra protection to the toes, but it also extends the life of the pointe shoes and provides traction.

To secure the ribbons to the shoe, fold the heel of the shoe forward over the insole and place the ribbon just beyond the crease, slightly angled toward the shoe tip. Fold the ribbon end over once to form a short hem, with the matte surface facing toward the foot. Then sew all the way around the ribbon edge with fairly small stitches, avoiding sewing over the pull string of the shoe. When tying the shoe, cross the ribbons high over the instep and wrap them twice around the ankle, immediately above the ankle bone. Knot the ribbons on the inner side of the ankle twice, and tuck the ends under the wrapped part. When putting on the shoes for the first time, you may find that the ribbons are too long. If so, wrap them around the ankle and knot them before you cut off the excess.

Additional protection against heel slippage can be gained by sewing elastic at the heel to wrap over the instep. In use, the elastic is partially hidden by the ribbons. However, if the shoe is properly fitted, this elastic will not be necessary. Many dancers protect against slippage by simply wetting the inside of the heel and rubbing a little rosin on it before putting on the shoes.

Parents can take certain preliminary measures to help prepare their child to dance on pointe comfortably. The skin of the dancer's toes must be hardened somewhat to withstand the inevitable rubbing within the shoes. A daily application of rubbing alcohol after a shower or bath will help toughen the skin of the toes. Another approach instead of hardening the skin is to put cream on your feet regularly to keep the skin supple and prevent blisters. As extra protection, a pad made of moleskin can protect areas that are most vulnerable, like the heel or the second toe (if it is longer than the big toe). Corn pads are also useful for protecting the second toe. If a blister develops, the area should be disinfected and the toe wrapped in moleskin. Moleskin, unlike regular bandages, does not have a pad in the middle; it adheres directly to the sore. It must be left in place until it falls off, about seven to ten days; your child can shower or take a bath with it on. The blister under the moleskin will heal in that space of time, and the bandage will peel off easily without hurting the skin. Moleskin can even be applied to broken skin, provided that the blister has been thoroughly disinfected.

HAIR

Securing the hair away from the face and neck allows a clear view of the neck area. The neck position permits teachers to make important alignment diagnoses, alerting them to problems further down the spine. Both girls and boys with long hair need to keep their hair off their face and neck. A headband or ponytail is usually sufficient for boys to achieve that goal. For girls, one of the easiest ways to deal with long hair is to braid it and then pin the braid up or secure it with barrettes. Another way of securing hair begins with a ponytail with a ribbon tied at the tip; the hair is rolled into a bundle until the elastic securing the ponytail is reached, then the ribbon is tied over the elastic. Any manner of putting the hair up for class is acceptable as long as the hair does not come down in class. Ultimately, students do not learn as well when they are distracted by hair falling all over their face.

A List of Necessities
Girls
> Tights
> Leotard
> Shoes
> Elastic hair bands, hairpins, ribbons for the hair
> Safety pins

Boys
> Tights
> Socks (if tights do not have feet)
> Shoes
> T-shirt or sweatshirt
> Dance belt (athletic belt)
> Headband or elastic bands for securing long hair

Add to the list (for both girls and boys) legwarmers or thick leggings if the weather is cool. In cool weather, an extra sweatshirt or sweater comes in handy until the body warms up. Additionally, if dancing on pointe, one should always have an extra pair of pointe shoes in his or her bag. Too often a pair of shoes will become too soft during class, or ribbons will come unsewn. The student will then have no choice but to sit out the remainder of the class.

Before buying any accouterments, check with the school to find out what its requirements or prohibitions may be. For example, if the floor in a studio is gray, which marks very easily, black shoes may not be allowed.

Dance clothes can be very expensive, and girls in particular are often seduced by all the frilly, soft items on sale in dance stores. It's best to know what clothing items are allowed in class before purchasing.

At the intermediate level, boys can benefit from a men's/boys' class to develop specific technical skills required of the male dancer. Student from the School of Madison Ballet, Madison, Wisconsin. © 2015 Maureen Janson

6

PARENT AND TEACHER RELATIONS

LOUIS XIV OF FRANCE UNDERSTOOD the value of ritual. Life at his court seemed to mirror the orderliness of a choreographed dance. From the moment he awoke (attended by courtiers and dignitaries invited to witness the event), throughout the day (during which his every encounter was governed by strict rules of etiquette) to his retirement in the evening (again formally escorted), Louis XIV sought to establish a harmonious atmosphere in which specific rules of conduct were applied to every exchange and encounter.

Observance of rituals remains an important part of the ballet world. The size of a major company may preclude a degree of familiarity that is often found in smaller groups; usually the ballet master or choreographer of the larger company is approached with formality, and a strict hierarchy among company members prevails. A dancer seldom questions the choreographer or teacher. Any complaints are filed through formal channels. The artistic director is in control of the artistic product; thus the management of a ballet company can be likened to the autocratic rule of a king.

This formal attitude toward the teacher or choreographer may be an anomaly in our culture today, yet there was a time when teachers were among the most respected members of our society. Both at the Paris Opera and at the Royal Ballet School, ballet students were expected to curtsy or bow to the teacher before and after class. Other cultures also preserve a certain decorum toward their mentors. In India the guru or dance teacher does not countenance questions. In his book *The Dance Through the Ages*, Walter Sorell quotes the Indian dancer Lalli as saying, "When I ask a question, Vikram affects good nature but reminds me that a student's question is a sign of little faith in the teacher."

ATTENDANCE AND PUNCTUALITY

In contrast to the state schools in Europe where students do not pay for instruction, open studios and private dance schools place the teacher in the position of having to please the students and parents. My teacher at the Paris Opera could refuse to allow students to participate in the class; the Paris Opera Ballet School is a state institution. Students accepted into the program attend without charge (although they pay for room and board) and are also beholden, under an unwritten contract, to fulfill their obligations: to attend classes, perform when required, and abide by the rules of the institution. In this country parents pay for the privilege of having their children instructed. However, too often they feel that this entitles them to take liberties.

The parent who drives the child to class is ultimately responsible for the child's punctuality. For the teacher to punish a tardy child by forbidding participation seems eminently unfair. However, this action is motivated by concern for the well-being of the student. Ballet class is a continuum, with each exercise following the previous one in a logical sequence that engages every muscle of the body cumulatively. The exercises are designed to warm the body gradually as well as impart kinetic information. A child who has missed the first couple of exercises has missed this information and runs the risk of injury by working with muscles that have not been properly warmed up. Therefore getting to class after it has started is not only discourteous and disruptive, but also robs the student of the opportunity to experience the technique in the logical manner in which it is presented.

Arriving on time has further benefit: it provides the opportunity to make an effective transition from the outside world of electronic devices, noise, and overstimulation to the meditative state of heightened self-awareness. Getting dressed for class becomes a part of the ritual, a moment of preparation that invokes the right frame of mind for sharing in the ritual of class fully and constructively. Punctuality allows the student to enter into a state of mind that is conducive to learning.

Punctuality is only one area where the parent sets the tone. A casual attitude on the part of the parent quickly communicates itself to the child and affects the way she or he accepts corrections, which has a direct impact on her or his progress. On the other hand, parents who regard the teacher as a professional who does not make up rules arbitrarily and who has the welfare of the child at heart, help to maintain the discipline necessary for their child's progress. The book *Beyond the Classroom* (1996), by Laurence Steinberg, Benson Brown, and Stanford Dornbusch, points to the indifference of parents as the main reason for underachievement in school. Children often reflect parental attitudes and priorities and unconsciously act them out. Furthermore, parents set criteria or expectations. "Did you have a good class?" elicits a different response than "Did you have fun?"

Learning to dance is a little different from learning how to play the piano or sing. In these disciplines, a weekly lesson is supported by individual practice. In dance, the lesson is both instruction and practice. Dancers need the vigilant eye of the teacher to catch departures from the desired line and to point out mistakes. Advanced dancers may on occasion do a barre on their own, but this is usually due to dire circumstances that prevent them from taking class. While a solitary barre warms the body and maintains the musculature, it is no substitute for regular class. In some ways, a missed class cannot be made up.

Especially in cases where an injury affects the student for a long time, the student should make an effort to observe classes. The benefit of this is absorbed by the student who is mature enough to learn from watching rather than doing. The advantages of watching class are numerous. Observation can provide new insights and understanding of the technique that can be applied when the student returns to class. It is easy to forget that dance is not only a physical activity, but an intellectual one as well. In an article called "The Mental Edge" (U.S News and World Report, August 3, 1992) William Allman writes: "In a study published this month, neurologist Scott Grafton of the University of Southern California found that the brain learns new skills by fine-tuning the neural circuits that are involved in making the motion." Thus going over a movement in your head helps to enhance the actual performance of the motion.

The idea that class cannot be missed and the need to observe when unable to participate were drummed into us from an early age. During my first semester at the Royal

Ballet School in London, all the new students were put under Miss Winifred Edwards's (1895–1989) tutelage. It was Miss Edwards's task to imbue us with the special Royal Ballet style, restrained yet regal, with clean technical definition.

Miss Edwards was a tall, forbidding person who wore white sandals and stood in a perfect fifth position. The process of learning seemed to us more like being broken in than being educated. Miss Edwards dismantled our little mannerisms, shortcuts, and adaptations, seeking a stark, precise execution of all movements. Besides teaching us technique, she lectured us on our diet and on how to take care of our equipment; our tunics were to be clean and pressed, and our shoes scrubbed with rubbing alcohol each week to erase dirt and scuffs. We also learned how to darn the tips of our pointe shoes to prolong their hardness and guard against slipping. Every Monday morning we stood in a row in front of Miss Edwards holding our supply of shoes out for her inspection, quaking lest our weekend scrubbing session appear to have been less than perfect.

Once, at the Royal Ballet School, I twisted my ankle coming down from a small jump. I returned to school to observe classes, hobbling with the aid of a cane. This time off proved invaluable. Not only did I sit in on the classes that I would regularly have attended, but I snuck in to observe other teachers. My favorites were Errol Addison (1903–1983) and Harold Turner (1908–1962). Mr. Addison, a small, jovial man, was a wonderful spinner and passed on the secrets of good pirouettes to his students. I had been a tentative turner at best, but after listening to Mr. Addison and watching his directives, I began to understand the dynamics of the motion. Mr. Turner was no less a showman, a little more distant and at times sarcastic. He always wore white to teach, his balding head gleaming as if freshly scrubbed. He was more precise technically than Addison was, but he still had a keen sense of drama and bravado. I returned to my own class with new enthusiasm, insight, and appreciation for the technique.

VOLUNTEER WORK AND STUDENT ADVANCEMENT

Many schools rely on the volunteer work of parents to organize a variety of adjunct activities. These may include printing programs and tickets, arranging refreshments for the intermission at performances, working at a reception desk during class sessions, or running fundraising events. I have asked several teachers how they feel about this, and their overwhelming response was that although they are grateful for the dedication and real help that such parents provide, they are also quick to remind that volunteer work does not entitle parents to dictate policy or interfere with the running of the school in any substantive way. However, teachers welcome input from parents when it concerns scheduling as well as individual problems that may arise.

While preprofessional ballet companies are generally nonprofit organizations, they still must be operated as businesses in the sense of keeping within a specified budget. Teachers like to hear comments, complaints, and concerns that allow them to provide a better service to their student body. Therefore, communication between teacher and parent is essential. When the need for a conversation arises, the best approach is to arrange an appointment when neither teacher nor parent will be rushed and the matter can be discussed in a congenial atmosphere.

Children studying dance are bound to feel disappointment at one time or another, perhaps because they did not get a part they wanted in a performance or were not placed in a higher-level class. Enid Lynn, director of the Hartford School of Ballet, says, "It is my hope that parents do not project their own disappointment to their children." She cites one incident when a mother insisted that because her daughter was not accepted into the preprofessional program, she would not return to the school. The child was heartbroken. In this case, the mother relented and brought the child to the open-enrollment program. Not every child is capable of becoming a professional, yet that is not valid reason to deny them dance classes. A child should have the opportunity to draw on the benefits of a dance education without the pressure of having to excel or commit to a career.

Parenting a young dancer requires delicate balance. At the other end of the scale from an overly ambitious parent is the one who constantly reminds the teacher in front of the child that the child is not going to be a dancer. At the same time, the parent demands steady improvement and perceivable hard work. The child in this case receives mixed messages: on the one hand the parent says that dance lessons are rather frivolous, but on the other hand the parent expects dedication and discipline. In one particular case, a child was very talented but also rather lazy. Because of the parent's attitude, the child progressed only because of innate ability and never reached her full potential.

Good teachers do not arbitrarily decide that one child should advance and another should not; they have the best interest of the child in mind when they make this kind of decision. It's best for parents to leave such decisions entirely up to the teacher. Children who are in the wrong class soon fall behind their classmates, class becomes a chore, and the most important aspect of dancing is lost: the pure joy of movement.

Some teachers are reluctant to accept students who have studied in other schools. They maintain that besides coming with all sorts of bad habits in the execution of the technique, if the student was dissatisfied at the previous studio she or he will eventually be dissatisfied with them, too. Although this attitude may seem extreme, and some students have a legitimate reason for switching teachers, there are instances when the move is motivated by reasons other than the welfare and education of the child. Most teachers will tell a parent when it is time to seek another teacher, generally because their program no longer provides what the child needs to progress.

For some reason, in the United States the idea taken hold that the more teachers the student studies with, the better. In the older traditions that are still followed in Europe and Russia, dancers study with one primary teacher for several years and may only have had a total of two teachers by the time they reach a preprofessional level. In professional schools, students study with a primary teacher and experience other teachers only when studying other subjects, like character dance or pointe.

The process of learning is always an active one. As a young, inexperienced teacher, I readily blamed the teacher for a student's bad technique. I have come to realize that the teacher can only present the material and insist on correct execution. I have often been humbled by students whose innate kinetic response was so beautiful that I could only gaze at them and wonder how they knew what they knew.

In several instances, I felt that an old dancer's soul was hiding in the young body; my role was to bring to consciousness all that the child already knew. A teacher, no matter how brilliant, cannot make a student into a dancer. Students bring into the studio their raw talent and active interest. The teacher provides the tools for fashioning an instrument—out of a sometimes unwilling body—that, with training, will become flexible, responsive, and graceful. It is the teacher's responsibility to provide the correct tools; a screwdriver will not do when a hammer is needed. The student's responsibility is to use the tool appropriately and to become ever more adept in its applications.

One of the most important ingredients in this process is trust. Both parent and child must trust that the teacher knows what is needed to ensure the child's progress. If you have doubts, ask questions, look at other studios, and change teachers if you are convinced that your teacher is not providing the necessary training. But blame for a child's lack of progress should not be placed arbitrarily on the teacher.

REHEARSALS

Probably the most difficult periods in the life of a studio are the weeks of rehearsal prior to a performance. During that time, patience and understanding must be exercised by all. Rehearsal is not like a class, with a definite structure and a prescribed set of movements to cover. Choreography has two stages: first, the learning of the steps, and second, the practice to perfect the dance. The dance is remembered and perfected only through repetition. Rehearsals may run overtime because any one section of the dance must be firmly fixed in the memory in order to be remembered at the next rehearsal. There is nothing more wasteful than to have students forget the material covered from one rehearsal to the next. This is like running on the same spot.

Once the students have committed the steps to memory, the real work of perfecting the dance begins. Perfecting the execution is an endless task; only through complete familiarity with the technical material can the spirit of the dance emerge. Additionally, every single performer is critical to the whole. In a group dance, performers rely on each other for the correct spacing; when students are missing, the others must imagine the space that would be occupied. This is a hard task, especially for neophytes.

The very format of rehearsals invites frayed nerves. Unlike class, rehearsals do not involve all dancers all of the time. Sitting out while a section is being completed may be boring, but the student must nevertheless sit quietly, without talking, so as not to distract either the choreographer or the other dancers. The cooperation of all participants, either active or passive, is essential to the smooth and efficient running of a rehearsal.

Even if your child is not considering a career in dance, the discipline of adhering to specific rules will establish a disciplined attitude toward other activities. The study of dance helps children become more studious students and more directed professionals in their chosen field.

In every situation, there is an appropriate behavior that suits the occasion. The process of educating children includes the recognition that we impose certain restraints on ourselves in order to function in the world. We do not, as a rule, allow our children to play hide-and-seek among the pews during a church service, or play basketball in the living room, or put their feet on the table during dinner. Rules established by society often disregard the individual expression in favor of communal comfort and safety. Similarly, the rules of behavior at dance studios are concerned with creating room for introspection in a receptive atmosphere.

In the barre exercises of a dance class every joint of the body should be gradually warmed, and all muscles stretched and strengthened, preparing the dancer for centre work. Students from the School of Madison Ballet, Madison, Wisconsin. © 2015 Maureen Janson

7

RECITALS, DEMONSTRATIONS, COMPETITIONS, AND CONCERTS

WHY PERFORM

Performance is often the main justification for all our hard work. In performance we realize truths that may escape us in the studio. The anticipation of performance keeps us interested, and the memory of the last performance sustains us and reinforces the necessity of keeping our instrument tuned. But is performing an essential part of the experience of learning to dance?

In short answer, yes. Performance completes our understanding of dance. It puts our long hours of practice into perspective and gives us an opportunity to share what we know and what we feel with others. It is a vital part of learning to dance because, through the experience, we learn how to draw pleasure by giving pleasure to others, and we nourish certain aspects of our personality that crave that kind of attention. Many dancers say that they feel most vital, most alive while dancing. Violette Verdy, speaking of Nureyev, said: "Maybe he did not get to the Absolute, but he kept going there ... His most purest, his everything was his dancing. Not because he was privileged, but because he gave everything."[1]

At the Paris Opera Ballet School, performance opportunities came early. We were cast as pages (walk-on parts) in operas and ballets. Operatic stories were our mythology, and to be part of the panoply was magic. During the day we were ordinary school children studying grammar and arithmetic; in the afternoon we attended ballet class and rehearsal; but in the evening, we stepped into a fairyland world of heroes.

My first role, at age eleven, was that of a page in Guiseppe Verdi's (1813–1901) *Otello*. I carried a casket of jewels to Desdemona, knelt in front of her as she sang her aria while admiring the jewels, and then retreated backward into the wings. I remember vividly the excitement of preparing for the performance—putting on the makeup and long blond wig—and standing quietly in the wings before stepping into the magical, lighted space. A silence of completion seemed to envelop me as I walked in measured steps toward Desdemona.

As we grew older, we were cast in walk-on parts in different operas. In some operas we actually danced: in Verdi's *Aida*, we were Blackamoors and then slaves in the Grand Procession; in Hector Berlioz's (1803–1869) *The Damnation of Faust*, we were Blessed Spirits, and then Devils. While the dance of the Devils was exciting, I preferred the dance of the Spirits, because the music was quietly evocative and our movements were soft, almost trancelike. My favorite opera was Charles Gounod's (1818–1893) *Romeo and Juliet*. Standing upstage, I marveled at Juliet's beauty as the chorus sang her praises in the first act, and I wept as she drank the poison in the third

---

[1] Interview with Russell D. Baker, University of Utah Department of Ballet Newsletter, Winter 1993.

act. The choreography in these works was designed for our competence, and one ballet was choreographed specifically for students, Albert Aveline's (1883–1968) *Jeux d'Enfants,* which was performed on special occasions.

The stage fueled my imagination, but I also learned an important lesson: to be fully accepting of my place within the whole; to realize, as the old cliché says, that there are no small parts. Every individual on stage fulfills an important role in the overall production, and the little girl kneeling for a few minutes at the feet of the diva is an integral part of the picture.

When major ballet companies come to the city, they sometimes require supers or extras, as they are known in the movies, to complete their productions. Students are often chosen for walk-on parts in *Swan Lake* or *Sleeping Beauty.* The experience is exciting and instructive, and the students invariably return to the studio newly inspired and motivated.

TYPES OF PERFORMANCES

Professional schools affiliated with a ballet company often mount a production of *The Nutcracker* in early winter. Well-established schools may have a junior company, composed of the most advanced students, that performs at social functions as well as at other schools and that mounts an occasional performance of its own. For many schools, however, an end-of-the-year recital is the only venue for performance. This recital serves several functions. It provides an opportunity for parents to see the student body in its entirety and to witness their child's progress within the larger context of other classes. It provides an outlet for the students' self-expression and a focus for the classwork. It is also a social occasion that brings parents together and engenders feelings of loyalty and support—a feeling of belonging to an exclusive club. Some schools participate in competitions, often traveling to other locations to perform before judges. How schools refer to the performance may indicate the breadth and formality of the presentation. Each of the common appellations—recital, demonstration, and concert—has a connotation that reveals its focus.

Recitals

Recitals vary both in scope and in length. Schools appreciate the fact that parents want to see their own children perform, and they try to provide every student with the opportunity for a solo. Generally the school rents an auditorium or theatre for the performance and, to offset the cost, charges parents a performance and a costume fee.

A serious drawback of the recital is that too often rehearsals take up class time beginning in the spring semester. While students are learning routines, they are not improving their technique; when half a year is spent on preparing for a performance rather than on regular study, the technical aspects of training are sadly neglected.

Nevertheless, the recital is popular with many schools as well as with parents and students, and it fulfills the need for performance experience.

Demonstrations

A demonstration usually describes a less formal presentation limited to showing the students' classwork. However, it is not an impromptu affair. The demonstration consists of material from the lessons that has been selected and arranged into a choreographed whole to represent what the students have been working on all year. It may also include some choreographed dances performed by the senior students as a finale.

As in the recital, each student is involved in the performance, and rehearsals may take place during regular class time. The demonstration does not typically detract from working on technique because the elements rehearsed are the same as those that would regularly be practiced. If the senior students are to perform a dance as a finale to the performance, it is usually rehearsed after the regular lesson is finished.

The format of the demonstration allows parents not only to see their own child's progress, but also to witness the progression of the technique through different levels. In many ways the demonstration is an educational experience for both parents and children. The students have the opportunity to see other classes and get some idea of where their training is leading them. The parents get an overview of the training their child is receiving and gain an appreciation of the technique as it unfolds through the years of study.

Another advantage of the demonstration is that it is usually a low-budget affair. While it may be necessary to rent an auditorium, the cost is generally covered by charging a modest ticket price. Also, there is no costume fee because the students perform in their classroom attire. The most significant advantage of the demonstration, however, is that it does not interrupt training to make time for rehearsals.

Concerts

A concert generally involves only the senior students of the school and is composed of choreographed works (usually short ballets). Some schools mount full-length productions of classics like *Coppélia* or *Cinderella*, which may provide an opportunity for all levels of students to participate. Rehearsals are scheduled separately from class time and often require the students to give up their weekends and many evenings.

Mounting a production requires many hours of work, not only in rehearsal time but in production time as well—designing and building the scenery, making the costumes, planning the lighting, arranging publicity and promotion. The group assembled for the duration functions as a professional company with a clear delineation of duties and responsibilities. The director of the school may commission a choreographer to mount the ballet or hire professional dancers for the principal roles. The experience for the students involved in such a production is invaluable. It duplicates the process of a professional company and allows the students to determine whether the life of a dancer is really what they want.

Although your primary reason for attending a presentation is to see your own child dance, every parent is there for the same reason. Your child may appear onstage only for a few minutes. The teacher's selection of the students is based on their proficiency, with an eye to creating a harmonious whole. For the child, the experience includes the anticipation and preparation for the performance, the excitement of waiting in the wings, and the applause at the end. Even if students are on stage for only two minutes, they will still experience the cumulative magic of the event.

Preprofessional Experience

Many schools establish performing groups to give their students an opportunity to gain performance experience at a preprofessional level. This experience is very valuable in the education of the dancer; it fosters the development of a stage presence and a firsthand realization of what being a dancer entails. In performance, the dancer realizes that technique is not enough; style and stage presence are also necessary. Performances need not be on a grand scale to be instructive. Whenever dancers step out in front of an audience—whether performing in a gym for elementary schoolchildren, or on a makeshift stage in a cafeteria for senior citizens—they are tapping into their artistic potential and transcending their technical levels.

A dancer must be able to communicate the enjoyment of motion to the audience. A technically brilliant performance without feeling leaves the audience cold. Ultimately such a performance, even with its amazing technical feats, is boring to watch. On the other hand, a technically flawed performance that is full of feeling may be a much more satisfying experience. Of course, we always hope for performances that are satisfying in both respects; brilliant technique becomes the vehicle for a full emotional expression.

Competitions

It has become popular for studios to subscribe to various competitions around the country. These competitions usually offer a weekend of master classes and workshops with distinguished teachers and culminate in performances by participating groups or individual dancers.

Studios that have a performing group often belong to the Regional Dance Association (RDA), formerly the National Association of Regional Ballet. The guidelines for membership in the association stipulate that the company must be a nonprofit organization separate from the school, it must have its own board of directors and a budget that is not tied to the operation of the studio, and it must present at least one major concert a year.

At the RDA's annual national conference, companies present works for adjudication. These judged competitions focus more on companies than on individual dancers, so many aspiring choreographers get their start by presenting works in this venue. For the student, this format removes much of the pressure and the sense of individual rivalry that can arise when solo performances are emphasized.

Established professional schools also have the option of attending international ballet competitions, which meet in places like Varna, Bulgaria (the site of the original competition); Lausanne, Switzerland; Jackson, Mississippi; and Paris. These competitions are highly publicized and require a very high level of proficiency on the part of the competitors. Dancers usually train for them throughout the year, practicing the required variations or pas de deux. These competitions, which focus on individual dancers, provide significant visibility to the dancers who qualify as finalists.

These venues provide additional performance experience, and the heightened pressures inherent in these situations often lead students to discover aspects of their personalities that were not apparent before: What is my response to pressure? Am I at my best when seriously challenged? Can I rise to the occasion, or do I want to run and hide?

Additionally, because these competitions attract dancers from all over the world, they provide an excellent forum for measuring one's own standard against an international norm.

Perhaps the most well-known of ballet competitions is the USA International Ballet Competition held every four years in Jackson, Mississippi. Reserved for dance students aged 15 and up, this prestigious event requires prescreening by way of a video application from all dancers wishing to compete. Award winners in both classical and contemporary divisions are granted the opportunity to perform in the gala concert.

Other competitions are open to younger dancers. For example, the World Ballet Competition held in Orlando, Florida has several age categories and allows dancers aged 10 and up to participate. Awards received by those who are judged on performance to be winner vary from money to scholarships to professional performance contracts.

While the competition performance is at the heart of these events, workshop and master class opportunities for those who travel to the location provide invaluable experiences.

COMPETITIVENESS

Dance is inherently competitive. Dancers will usually compare themselves to others in the class and strive to emulate or challenge themselves to better those who possess qualities that they feel they lack. This type of healthy competition spurs the students to excel and improve. However, when competition is actively encouraged by the studio or the parent, it begins to act as a barrier between students and their classmates and breeds an unsuitable atmosphere.

We are not always chosen for the part we covet; casting in the annual production may cause some heartaches. It helps to remember that casting is less an expression of favoritism than a judgment call. Negative feelings toward

the teacher or the classmates only interferes with the learning process and robs the children of their power and will to
improve.

My daughter, Nadia, still remembers vividly an incident
that occurred when she was 11 and danced in the annual production of *The Nutcracker*. That year she had been selected
as one of the eight little Pulcinellas who emerge from under
the skirt of Mother Goose. She was very excited because this
was a real dancing part. During one of the performances, the
bonnet of Mindy, the girl next to her, became untied and, in
the course of the dance, fell off. Mindy let it fall, finished the
dance, and had the presence of mind to pick up the hat on
her way offstage. She acted like a good little pro. But Mindy's
mother, greeting the girls backstage, started screaming at
Nadia, accusing her of deliberately knocking the hat off.
Mindy started crying, Nadia started crying, and the mother
went on screaming. Nadia believed she had indeed ruined
the performance, and she felt guilty and hurt. This experience overshadowed all the other happy performances in
which she had taken part.

The mother of a young dancer once confided in me that
there were two reasons why she transferred her daughter
from a popular studio to another one: "The students were
not getting enough attention because the classes were so
big. Even worse, there was such competitiveness among
the mothers. They will tell you the wrong time or day for
an audition just so that their daughter will get a better
chance."

While competitiveness is an unavoidable part of learning to dance, when it is encouraged by teachers or parents, it
begins to distract from the real work of learning and growing
within the art form.

BALANCE BETWEEN
PERFORMANCE AND CLASS

In order to perform, we must first rehearse. During the training years, a balance must be maintained between rehearsing and training. Rehearsal is not a substitute for class. Before the student reaches an intermediate level, she or he cannot miss classes because there are too few. When the student reaches an intermediate level she or he needs to be engaged in practicing and perfecting the technique on a daily basis; two or three classes a week are no longer sufficient for progress. Simply maintaining technique at one level is rather frustrating; it's like treading water. Your head stays above the waves, but you are not getting anywhere. The daily class provides an opportunity to integrate new concepts and to perfect well-known ones. It is only through daily practice that one can achieve a high level of proficiency.

An amazing fact of the craft is that a dancer can perform a simple motion, such as a battement tendu—which is only a stretching of the leg with the toes and instep ending in an arched position—and after forty years of practice still discover new features to the motion, new sensations to be integrated. The technique is extremely complex in its simplicity, but its breadth and depth are available to us only through practice. Therefore, every year of the student's dance studies is crucial to the correct development of her or his kinetic and intellectual understanding within the dance.

There is an old adage in the profession: If you miss one class, you know it; if you miss two classes, your teacher knows it; if you miss three classes, your public knows it. Schools that substitute rehearsals for classes, while obviously preparing well for the coming production, are in fact denying young dancers the opportunity to maintain their technique, let alone progress. While the experience of performing is a very important component of dance education, providing insights for technical growth and allowing the dancer to gain confidence and develop stage presence, rehearsal schedules must honor the requirements of the daily class and not act as a substitute. In dance companies the day begins with class and only then proceeds to rehearsal. On performance days, when time is limited and dancers need their strength for the evening show, class takes precedence. The first years of training lay the foundation for a solid technique; the last years of training are equally vital in developing technique and preparing the dancer for the challenges of the professional world. In fact, even labeling those years as the last years of training is misleading. Dancers are in training throughout their careers, so a balance must always be maintained between performance and class.

Learning to enjoy the process is an integral part of learning to dance. The process consists of little steps, small triumphs, and small challenges, and progress is based on the gradual improvement in execution. Students from the School of Madison Ballet, Madison, Wisconsin. © 2015 Maureen Janson

8

AVOIDING INJURIES

BALLET HAS BEEN MUCH MALIGNED as injurious to the body. Rotating the legs in turnout and the redistribution of weight ballet requires do put unusual strains on the body. Yet even the repetition of recreational swimming puts strain on the body. Most forms of exercise do. Furthermore, the warm-up process is an integral part of dance training.

Young children do not generally sustain injuries by taking dance classes. It is only in more advanced training, when the musculature has been developed and dancers push the limits of their physicality, that problems may arise. However, early training conditions the musculature to a specific response. Correct use of the musculature from the start makes the dancer less prone to injury in later years.

Other factors that can also make a dancer susceptible to injury include improper diet, lack of rest, surrounding conditions like extreme cold and heat, and even emotional state. Through proper diet, muscles receive the nourishment they need to function efficiently and safely, and rest helps the body to perform at its peak. Surrounding conditions cannot always be controlled, but they must be addressed with proper attire and a careful warm-up period when it is very cold. Part of the discipline of dancing is the learned ability to leave problems at the door of the studio, so dancers must also learn to transcend their emotional state. By paying full attention to the task at hand dancers will not only avoid the risk of injury, but may also find that their minds are clearer and better able to cope with negative issues after the class is over.

CORRECT TECHNIQUE

Most dance injuries are caused by misalignment or incorrect execution of the technique, which over time predispose the body to injury. When first selecting a school, parents should watch for a few signs that correct technique is being taught. Are the students standing straight, and does the teacher correct them when they are not? Correct spinal alignment keeps the natural curves in place. The spine has an inward curve at the lumbar area (lower back), a slight natural rounding near the shoulders, and another slight inward curve at the neck. These curves are present when the students stand straight. Does the teacher guide them to keep the shoulders and hips aligned to each other, and is the head balanced over the body (with the chin neither tucked under nor thrust upward)?

Does the teacher emphasize turnout from the hips and correct the students who are rolling over on their instep (pronation, a sure sign that the student is not turning out from the hips)? Pronation is the cause of many problems, including knee pain and shinsplints. Are the students taught to keep their knees over their feet when bending the knees? Does the teacher talk about alignment and line, or is the height of the leg in extensions emphasized without regard to alignment and line?

It is undeniable that some body types are better suited to dance; they have a wide range of motion as well as an innate strength that allows them to control their motions from an early age. For the majority of others whose physique falls short of the ideal, it is important to recognize limitations and work with them intelligently. People with short ligaments approach the stretching process with care in order to lengthen the ligaments as they build stronger muscles to protect the joints; people with long ligaments have a wider range of motion, so they exercise care in keeping aligned in order to maintain the integrity of the joints and build strength and control. The teacher's corrections will indicate how concerned he or she is with the issues of alignment and correct execution and, most importantly, with the specific needs of each student. Does the teacher demand the same degree of turnout from all students, or does he or she correct them individually according to their capability?

SURROUNDING CONDITIONS

While injury in the studio is not common with young children, the proper surroundings during the early years of training will enhance the learning experience. Muscles function better in a warm environment. Most studios are warm in the winter; if windows are opened, care should be taken that the cooler air does not blow directly on the students. In the summer, if air conditioning is used, the thermostat ideally will not be set below 78 degrees. The process of warming up is hampered by cool temperatures, and the muscles contract quickly when idle; therefore, a warm studio is healthier for dancers in both winter and summer. Humid conditions can also lead to muscle cramps.

Surrounding conditions also include the floor. The surface should provide traction without being sticky, a nonslip material such as Marley (linoleum is not suitable, as it is usually too slippery) or wood that has been treated with a finish that prevents slipping. Rosin is sometimes used on wooden floors but is not always necessary on Marley. Wetting the shoes is also a solution when dancing on a polished wood floor. The floor must also be sprung; Marley laid over a concrete surface is not suitable. The importance of a sprung floor cannot be overestimated. Many injuries are caused by jumping on an unyielding floor.

Suitable barres are also essential to a well-equipped studio. The height of the barre should be set at waist level. Most studios have a double rung of barres to accommodate both tall and short students; these should be securely fastened to the walls. Free-standing barres are also suitable as long as they are very sturdy. Many styles and designs of free-standing barres are used. One of the best kinds is the home-made model made out of lengths of heavy pipes (found in plumbing supply stores); lighter material, such as aluminum, does not provide enough support. These considerations will contribute to the students' comfort and greatly reduce the risk of injury.

COMMON DANCE INJURIES AND TREATMENT OPTIONS

Most doctors are not aware of the type of exercise that ballet training entails, and they often simply tell the patient not to dance. If your child sustains an injury and is advised to stop dancing for a period of time, explain to or show the doctor some ballet exercises and determine together whether they are indeed injurious or whether they would facilitate recovery. Physical therapy is usually recommended after an injury; in many instances the ballet class can become part of the rehabilitation process. Talk to the dance teacher, explain the nature of the injury and the recommendation of the doctor, and with that information the teacher can select the types of exercises that the student needs to avoid. In many cases, it is not necessary to stop dancing altogether.

As the field of dance medicine continues to gain a presence within traditional Western medicine, treatment options are evolving to be specific to and more appropriate for dancers and the common injuries that can occur. An increasing number of trained dancers enter the physical therapy realm as a second career track. Finding a medical professional with dance experience can be a great benefit in recognizing and treating dance injuries. If a dance medicine professional is not available, often a sports medicine orthopedic can understand the demands of dance more than one who is not familiar with the physicality of ballet training.

There are two types of injuries: traumatic and chronic. The first is the result of a mishap, like twisting an ankle or pulling a muscle. The second type often follows the first; for example, if a dancer strains the Achilles tendon and does not allow it enough time to heal, he or she may develop tendonitis. A chronic condition such as tendonitis may also develop through habitually incorrect usage of the technique, such as not putting the heels down in jumps (which, again, affects the Achilles tendon).

In all cases, the first step to treating any injury should be to seek the advice of a medical professional. It's wise to rest the injured area until a treatment plan has been devised, as any injury is unique to the individual and will have its own appropriate care. A treatment plan will also depend upon the injury (its location on the body, and whether it is acute or chronic), and the medical advice that you seek.

Strains

A strain is damage to a tendons or muscle. Strains are basically pulled muscles, and vary in severity. Although they can be very painful, professional advice often encourages the patient to remain mobile. It is best to gently work through a muscle strain, making sure that the muscle is not overworked and that other parts of the body are not stressed in compensation. However, when a tendon is strained, the severity of the injury determines its treatment. If the tendon is strained at its juncture with the muscle, the condition is less severe than when the tendon is pulled at its insertion into the bone. In this case greater care in rehabilitation needs to be taken, and immobility may be recommended. In very severe cases surgery is sometimes needed to reattach the tendon.

Inflammation of the tendon is called tendonitis and requires initial rest. The most vulnerable tendon for dancers is the Achilles tendon. However, most dancers work through tendonitis, avoiding motions and positions that cause pain, and when the Achilles tendon is injured, limiting rises on half-pointe and jumps. Icing after a workout is recommended, as the Achilles is a slow area to heal.

Sprains

A sprain is damage to a ligament. Sprains are potentially more serious than strains because ligaments are inelastic.

Ligaments stabilize the joints, and because ligaments have a poor supply of blood, the healing process is slow. Sprains are often accompanied by strains because of the damage to surrounding tissues.

Sprains can be caused by misalignment when destabilizing pressure is routinely placed on an area. In this case, the dancer will probably have experienced discomfort for some time and will need to pay attention to the usage of the affected joint. Sprains can also be the result of injury, such as twisting an ankle or knee. Although accidents do occur in dance classes, they are usually the result of improper alignment; therefore, the previous advice still holds true: attention to alignment is the best prevention. It is usually advisable to see a doctor when a sprain occurs to determine the degree of injury and to make sure no fracture has been sustained. Partial or total immobilization may be recommended for a time; however, the treatment of injuries continues to evolve, and doctors are not as likely as they once were to advise complete immobility or the use of crutches. The doctor may initially advise rest and elevation, and then encourage motions that do not hurt in order to regain mobility of the joint. In the case of some injuries ice can be applied immediately to the affected area, although the effectiveness of ice to reduce inflammation has met with recent criticism. Ice and heat used alternatively can help relieve soreness in muscles, preventing a muscle from going into a chronic "holding pattern." Many dancers do routinely ice their muscles before retiring to bed.

Dislocation

Dislocation is not common in ballet dancers. However, should it occur, the intervention of a doctor is necessary to replace the joint. Tissue around the affected joint will have been traumatized, so the rest of the treatment follows the guidelines for sprains and strains. If a child is prone to dislocations, the affected area can be strengthened with physical therapy and special attention to alignment when dancing.

Shinsplints

A shinsplint is a microscopic tearing of ligament fibers in the lower leg away from their point of origin. Like strains and sprains, shinsplints are often caused by misalignment (which includes pronation) or dancing on dance floors that are too hard, and can even be the result of wearing shoes that either are too heavy or have heels of an unusual height. They can even be caused by walking too fast, or by doing too much during a first class after a vacation. The usual treatment for shinsplints is ice, compression, and taping the affected area for added support. If a child complains of shinsplints over an extended period of time, a secondary condition may have arisen; a visit to the doctor and X-rays may be necessary to determine that there are no hairline fractures.

Fractures

Fractures occur in bones. All fractures are severe and require the intervention of a doctor. Only ice should be applied immediately after this type of injury occurs, not heat; heat will only increase inflammation. The area must not be massaged, as this may cause further damage. Diagnostic X-rays are important: while massaging may help a strained muscle, it will only cause further damage to a fracture. If the fracture must be cast, the length of time that the limb is in a cast will determine the length of the rest period required. Usually a period of rehabilitation is necessary after a cast is removed. Removable casts allow mobility to enter the rehab process sooner than with traditional plaster casting. Although a fracture is always serious and may take a long time to heal, it is not fatal to a career. With proper rehabilitation, the dancer can return to her or his craft in time.

Pain-Causing Conditions

A condition common in athletically active girls is the Osgood-Schlatter's disease, which affects children between the ages of 12 and 16. This condition is associated with growth spurts in the tibia and causes pain in the knees. Despite its frightening appellation, Osgood-Schlatter is a condition that children outgrow. Nevertheless, a child chronically suffering with knee pain should see an orthopedic doctor, preferably one who specializes in sports medicine. The degree of pain experienced and the threshold of pain that the person can withstand will determine how the condition will affect the dancer. Some people anticipate pain while others tend to ignore it; the latter are more successful in working through this condition. Some students have given up dancing once this condition was diagnosed, but others have successfully worked through it.

Another common condition is scoliosis, which is a lateral curvature of the spine. Adolescent children are often tested for this condition, which varies in severity from a slight curve to one that may affect the alignment of the pelvis. Scoliosis has been recorded to occur in upward of four percent of the population, although most of us have some sort of spinal asymmetries. Dancing can help realign the vertebrae through the tensile strength of the surrounding musculature. If your child has been diagnosed with scoliosis, sharing that information with the teacher will enable him or her to exert extra vigilance in correcting your child's alignment.

Except in extremely severe cases, where a brace or surgery is necessary, scoliosis need not be treated as an impairment. The very nature of ballet training—working both sides of the body equally and in harmony—can help to correct the misalignment that scoliosis creates.

Pain and Compensation

Pain is the body's signal that tissue is damaged. It should not be ignored. On the other hand, because dancers work their bodies with such intensity, some degree of pain is habitually experienced. However, there is a difference between the pain of an overused, tired muscle and one that has been injured. Pain from overuse is usually dull, and will feel better after a hot bath or a gentle massage. An injury can be initially accompanied by a sharp pain and often by muscular spasms around the affected area. Because there is no way of knowing immediately the severity of an injury, the steps mentioned earlier are recommended: placing a call to the appropriate medical professional, resting the area, possibly icing and elevating the injury, and avoiding massage. Your doctor may recommend X-rays, or in some cases an MRI (magnetic resonance imaging, which shows greater detail than an X-ray) should be taken to determine the nature and extent of the injury.

The body has wonderful resources that come into play when an injury occurs. One of those resources is called "splinting": the muscles around an injury harden in order to protect from further trauma. Anyone who has been injured has experienced the slow localization of pain: at first a wide area seems to be affected, but as the healing process goes on, the area of pain shrinks to the point of the actual injury. After the injury has been diagnosed and the swelling has gone down, massage and stretching may be prescribed in order to relieve the muscular spasm associated with splinting. Another problem can also arise that dancers need to be acutely aware of after an injury: the body compensates for its inability to fully use the injured area by utilizing other muscles and joints for the same tasks. This compensation may create problems of its own; when a dancer comes back to class after an injury, she or he must be sure to work the body equally without favoring the injured area.

Dancers rely on muscle memory to perform the increasingly complex motions of the technique, but muscles also retain the memory of trauma, both physical and psychic. When I was 13, I fell onto a spike and gashed out a sizable hole in my left quadricep. Months later I met one of the therapists who had worked with me. He asked me how I was feeling, and I said fine. Then he said "Why are you limping?" I was totally unaware of the compensation that my body had set up and that no longer served any purpose.

HELPING THE BODY TO RECOVER

The body can be likened to an automobile engine. The body of a dancer is a very sophisticated instrument, like a Rolls-Royce engine. Maintenance of such an engine must also be sophisticated. Therefore, when seeking medical help you must find the people who have the most experience with soft tissues, muscles, and bones. Sports doctors who are knowledgeable about dance, orthopedic doctors (particularly those who have specialized in dance), osteopaths, chiropractors, physical therapists, and acupuncturists have the expertise necessary to help diagnose problems and prescribe correct treatments. Applied kinesiologists and massage therapists are especially sensitive to the problems of dancers and can provide the supplemental care needed for complete rehabilitation.

Proper nutrition can aid in body recovery. Substances containing caffeine should be avoided, if for no other reason than to allow the injured dancer to sleep routinely. A list of things to eliminate can include coffee, tea, chocolate, and soft drinks containing caffeine. Sugar substitutes should be avoided. The chemicals often found in food additives end up being stored in the muscles and affect their ability to repair and renew. Water flushes out the impurities in the system and helps the body heal itself, so drinking plenty of it is helpful. Breathing deeply brings needed oxygen, which also plays a part in the healing process. It is difficult to stop the panic after you have sustained an injury, but panic and fear also interfere with healing.

A balanced diet, a regimen of breathing exercises (such as that which some yoga techniques provide), enough rest and sleep, and attention to alignment in dance classes will go a long way in preventing injuries. But should an injury occur, it must be remembered that the doctor is not a magician; he or she needs the patient's cooperation if the healing is to be successful. Furthermore, suffering from aches and pains has to be accepted as a part of any physical discipline. In dance, when the muscles are constantly stretched and flexed, a certain amount of lactic acid builds up and causes temporary stiffness and a mild ache. This is not a sign of injury, but one of intense use; the cure is to go on dancing in class. This difference between aches and pains should be noted. As the body warms up, the aches disappear. It is only when the pain persists that there is reason to be concerned about a possible problem. If repeated injuries are sustained or a chronic condition has developed, such as tendonitis or bursitis, the execution of the technique may be at fault. Analyzing alignment and the way specific motions are performed within ballet technique is part of the solution. Cross-training through the Feldenkrais, Alexander, and Pilates techniques provide that sort of analysis and are methods that can recondition the body for continued efficient use of the musculature.

As young professional students at the Paris Opera School, we were forbidden to engage in any athletic activity outside of dance class. Ice skating, horseback riding, and even team sports like volleyball were off-limits. The reason given for this edict was that sports build muscles that are not desirable for dancers, and, additionally, expose you to the risk of injury. When a child becomes serious about dance and considers it as a career, she or he is advised to avoid sports. A strained knee or ankle is a momentary impediment to most people, but for dancers it becomes a serious setback. Swimming has become a widely practiced and acceptable sport for dancers when used for its aerobic conditioning value rather than as a serious competitive pursuit.

Make sure that your studio has a first aid kit, including some ice or a supply of ice packs, and some athletic tape or Ace bandages. For those on pointe, carrying some moleskin and bandaids in a dance bag can be helpful. Prevention is always the best policy. A balanced diet, enough rest, working with an aligned body, and avoiding activities that are inherently risky should ensure an injury-free experience in dance.

Excellent books on dance-related injuries cover this subject in more depth: *Preventing Dance Injuries*, 2nd edition, edited by Ruth Solomon, Sandra C. Minton, and John Solomon (2005); *Dancing Longer Dancing Stronger*, by Andrea Watkins and Priscilla M. Clarkson (1994); and *Finding Balance: Fitness, Training, and Health for a Lifetime in Dance*, by Gigi Berardi (2005), provide details on injury prevention and longevity of dance life.

Every every day dancers face their image in the mirror, and every motion, every line of the body, comes under scrutiny. Students from the School of Madison Ballet, Madison, Wisconsin. © 2015 Maureen Janson

9

DIET AND EATING DISORDERS

WE LIVE IN A DIET-CONSCIOUS age and are subjected, on an almost daily basis, to new discoveries of the properties of food. We know a great deal about nutrition, especially which foods to avoid, and we appreciate the connection between nutrition and health. Often difficult to weed out the good from the bad when it comes to the plethora of information about food on the Internet, common sense and looking toward a balanced diet are the best ways to maintain overall health. Nevertheless, the looming presence of fast food restaurants, the convenience of grabbing lunch from a vending machine, and the constant invention of new processed foods (which are sometimes falsely marketed as being healthy) leads us as a nation to persist in all sorts of destructive eating habits.

Just as we go overboard in our indulgences, so we can also become fanatical about our diets. As the parent of a young dancer, it's wise to be aware of the types of stress that are associated with the profession: the emphasis on thinness; the concern with and acute awareness of the shape of the body; and, too often, a disparaging attitude toward achievements. These stresses sometimes contribute to push an otherwise healthy child into experimenting with food. For a dancing child, eating less than siblings is common because the dancer is more concerned with the body. Awareness is, in many ways, a survival tactic. Body image in dance is slowly changing—broadening to accept physical types beyond cookie-cutter thinness or specific heights. Yet it remains largely the norm that to succeed in the dance world, a dancer has to maintain an optimum weight. This awareness also makes dancers more prone to all sorts of extremes in their diets.

While being overweight is not healthy, an obsession with thinness may be even worse. Young dancers model themselves on mature artists without realizing that the streamlining depends on age and training as much as it does on the right diet. If proper nourishment is not obtained during the growing years growth may be stunted, or stopped altogether, and level of energy will diminish. Willful malnutrition may have serious physical and medical repercussions in later years.

The best advice I have heard on this topic came from a doctor after the birth of my first child. He said, "Eat everything in small amounts, never have seconds, avoid sweets, and never eat between meals" Within three months, I was back to the weight I had been before the pregnancy, and the extra weight stayed off.

Awareness of what and how much is good for us is the first step toward a balanced diet. The percentages of daily dietary need established by the American Heart Association, the National Academy of Sciences, and the National Institutes of Health, are roughly 55 percent carbohydrates, 15 percent protein, and 30 percent fat.

A sedentary child requires lower caloric intake than an active child, and as the child ages, the calories necessary to maintain weight and energy go up. For example, in a 2010 report, the US Department of Agriculture and the US Department of Health and Human Services recommend that a moderately active female between the ages of 9 and 13 requires 1600 to 2000 calories a day. (A male of the same age group and activity level should consume between 1800 and 2200 calories daily.)

Recent studies suggest that especially for physically active people and growing children, the 55 percent of carbohydrates may be excessive; more protein in the diet would be beneficial. Yet the same 2010 report suggests that the type of carbohydrate is important, stating that "many people consume too much added sugar and refined grain and not enough fiber." Although fiber has no nutritional value, it is a necessary component of any diet because it aids digestion. Fiber can be found in most vegetables and unrefined grains.

DIETARY ELEMENTS

Carbohydrates

Complex carbohydrates are composed of sugars, starches, minerals, vitamins, and some protein. Broken down by our digestive system, they provide the fuel we need. Complex carbohydrates include potatoes, pasta, bread, rice, corn, and a variety of vegetables and legumes. In macrobiotic cooking beliefs, brown rice is seen as a bone-strengthening important carbohydrate and should be consumed every day.

Protein

Protein has long been considered the major source of energy; it feeds our muscles. Complete protein products include all meats and dairy foods; however, dairy foods such as cheese have a higher percentage of fat than most meats.

Fat

A misapprehension of the function of fat has led some people to eliminate it almost entirely from their diet. Fat is a necessary dietary component, ensuring healthy skin and hair and aiding in the absorption of fat-soluble vitamins, such as A, D, E, and K. Yet as the child grows, less fat is needed for a healthy balance. The body produces its own saturated fats, which serve important functions, so there is no need to supplement a diet with saturated fats such as coconut oil or butter. Our systems make better use of polyunsaturated fats such as sunflower or canola oil.

Balancing a Diet

Dietary needs change as we grow older. A growing child who is building bones needs more protein than an adult. Additionally, dancers need more protein than less active people to help muscles repair and rebuild. But it is also a fact that dance is not an aerobic activity, and dancers do not burn as many calories as do athletes who are engaged in an aerobic activity. (Some studios encourage and sometimes provide an aerobic program for their students.) If a person's metabolic rate is slow, dancing will not change it; she or he has either to engage in an activity, such as walking or swimming laps, that will speed metabolism, or to limit food intake.

Reducing calorie intake by following a balanced diet that will provide between 1200 and 1500 calories includes:

Carbohydrates: 4 portions. One portion equals one slice of bread (preferably whole-wheat), one cup of dry cereal, one cup of pasta or rice, or one small baked potato.

Vegetables and fruit: 4 portions. One portion equals one piece of fruit or one cup of raw or cooked vegetables.

Lactose: 2 portions for adults, 4 portions for adolescents. One portion equals eight ounces of milk, eight ounces of low-fat yogurt, one ounce of cheese, or one cup of cottage cheese.

Protein: 2 portions. One portion equals four ounces of meat, poultry, or fish, or one cup of beans.[1]

A typical day with a diet of this kind may look like this:

Breakfast: a bowl of cereal with eight ounces of low-fat milk, a piece of fruit, and a piece of whole-wheat toast or a muffin.

Lunch; a small salad or a bowl of soup, a turkey or tuna sandwich, and a piece of fruit.

Snack: a choice of two items: carrot sticks, a piece of fruit, raisins, yogurt, a couple of whole-wheat cookies or crackers.

Dinner: meat (a small steak, chicken breast or thigh, or fish filet); pasta or potatoes; green beans, spinach, or zucchini; a small green salad; and bread.

A diet that includes more protein would allow more meat, fish, or poultry and less bread, pasta products, potatoes, and corn (corn is extremely high in sugar content and should generally be avoided). This type of diet would increase the protein intake to three portions and reduce the carbohydrates and vegetables/fruit to two portions each.

---

[1] Adapted from Allan J. Ryan, MD, and Robert E. Stephens, PhD, *The Healthy Dancer*, Princeton, NJ: Princeton Book Company, 1989, p. 85.

Here are a few ideas to consider in maintaining or regaining control over what and how much to eat:

1. Establish a regimen of three or four meals a day, eaten at approximately the same time every day.
2. How much you eat is as significant as what you eat. Resist having seconds. (Cheating by piling food on the plate in anticipation of not being allowed seconds will not help the desired outcome.)
3. Have a variety of foods every day.
4. Love what you eat. Pay attention while eating every item on the plate.
5. Listen to your needs. Sometimes a craving for a particular food indicates a deficiency of a particular vitamin or mineral. (Candy bars are excluded!)
6. Stick to eating meals only, with nothing in between. Avoid snack foods such as potato chips, cookies, manufactured snacks, etc.
7. Eliminate adding sugar to tea or coffee.
8. Learn the difference between hunger and turning to food because you are bored or upset.
9. If you must snack, make it fruit or yogurt; both will provide more lasting energy than a candy bar.
10. Avoid food with preservatives.

A survey of the diets of the dancers at one school suggested they keep a record of everything they ate for one week. Only a few had regular meals with their families. The majority ate sandwiches, fast food takeouts and snack foods. This little test lead to a discussion and increased awareness on balanced diets and the impact that an adequate regimen has on energy level, ability to concentrate, and general well-being.

Sitting down to a meal, no matter how modest, is a ritual that transcends the mere intake of food for survival. Breaking bread with those you love is an acknowledgment and celebration of the bonds that unite you. Preparation of that food, which need not be elaborate, is very much part of that ritual. Eating assumes a rightful place in the rhythm of life, and food nourishes the soul as well as sustains the body.

EATING DISORDERS

In talking about dancers, we cannot avoid the subject of eating disorders. The National Eating Disorders Association has found that many teen athletes can fall prey to food issues. Dancers are particularly susceptible because the milieu in which they work demands and rewards thinness, and because their character profile closely matches the general profile of people who are prone to this condition.

Dancers live and work in a highly autocratic milieu. The more accomplished dancer continues to learn through being criticized, with little if any positive reinforcement of their talent. The result can be not only a poor self-image but an over-reliance on the opinion of the mentor. Dancers may not trust their own perceptions, and thus tend to develop a warped self-image; seeing fat where there are only bones is only one aspect of this. Every morning male and female dancers alike, face their image in the mirror, and every motion, every line of the body comes under scrutiny, both their own and the teacher's. They pass judgment, a judgment that has been formed by looking at their fellow dancers and an often unrealistic, imagined ideal. (For a thoroughly enlightening discussion of this subject, see Dr. L. M. Vincent's *Competing with the Sylph*, 1980).

In her book *Dancing on My Grave* (1986), Gelsey Kirkland, former ballerina with the New York City Ballet and American Ballet Theatre, says:

> Mr. Balanchine's ideal proportions called for an almost skeletal frame, accentuating the collarbones and length of the neck. Defeminization was the overall result, with frequent cessation of the menstrual cycle due to malnutrition and physical abuse. . . . Many of the excesses of American ballet seem to be the result of the slimness trend, turning the ideal of beauty into mere fashion. Mr. B pushed us in that direction, but he also popularized ballet. This offers the hope that the public may press for reform—as an increasing number of ballet parents become concerned for the welfare of their children. (p. 56)

Some doctors believe that some people may have a genetic and or physiological predisposition to eating disorders. The psychological profile seems to play a central role: typically, anorexics are perfectionists—meticulous, scholarly, and compliant. These same qualities are shared by many dancers who continually strive to please mentors or parents and, in the process, fail to develop their own individuality.

A low level of self-esteem and a distorted perception of physical appearance are, according to psychiatrists, only the tip of the iceberg. Some people are medically or socially predisposed to slip into anorexia. Slipping into the condition may be a very apt way of describing its onset. The disorder actually begins with an obsession with food. As one dancer describes it: "I read about food; I dreamed about food; I thought about food. I knew the exact caloric content of every type of food,

I had set my limit at 1000 calories. A slice of bread and cheese amounted to 300 calories, I would say 'I can't have that, it will put me over my limit.'" She subsisted on a salad for lunch and a bowl of popcorn for dinner. Her energy level dropped and she stopped menstruating, yet every time she looked in the mirror she saw her imperfections and felt that her only recourse was to lose more weight.

Kate Thomas, director of the School at Steps Dance School in New York City, feels that she and her staff would not accept an underweight dancer into their program. A dancer needs to be at a healthy weight in order to pursue a dance career, and that in some cases, that knowledge can trigger healthier eating habits.

Dancers are not the only people who suffer from eating disorders. We need only look around us to see the large number of overweight people in this country. Extreme thinness is less detectable because we admire it in our culture, pursue it with diets and exercise, and compliment each other when we lose a few pounds. Although eating disorders often affect girls in their prepubescent and adolescent years, they are not limited to that age group and can claim victims of both sexes and all ages; however, between 85 and 90 percent of people suffering from anorexia and bulimia are women. The onset of these disorders typically occurs between the ages of 12 and 18 but can occur later. Anorexia and bulimia are characterized by an obsessive fear of being fat, bolstered by an unrealistic self-image; individuals perceive themselves as fat when they are in fact normal or even underweight.

Talking with dancers about weight elicits many similar stories. We have all stood in front of the mirror in the dressing room and pointed to our hips or buttocks, seeing the piece of chocolate consumed in a weak moment the previous night. Most of us have experimented with crazy diets in which black coffee and carrots, grapefruit, or milk and bananas provide the only sustenance for days. Some of us have even taken laxatives in the belief that the food we consumed would move through our systems much faster and therefore would not turn to fat. Fortunately, most of us have outgrown these adolescent obsessions and do not have a chronic weight problem, although we go on watching what and how much we eat.

Between the ages of fourteen and twenty, the female body begins to fill out as the girl becomes a woman. Unfortunately, this period also corresponds to a time of intense training and, for some, entrance into the professional world. Therefore, the onset of womanhood is sometimes perceived not as a natural evolution but as a threat. This is further complicated in the ballet world by the notion that an ideal figure for a ballerina should be extremely thin and sylphlike. Balanchine championed a group of so-called baby ballerinas in the 1930s and 1940s whose preadolescent body types became the norm for many performers. Thus, a young girl who is developing a figure may starve herself to maintain her prepubescent look.

Those prone to anorexia starve themselves; they eat small portions of food or sometimes stop eating altogether. Their bodies do not receive enough nourishment to sustain normal functions. The menstrual cycle is interrupted, because it depends upon a certain percentage of fat in the body to function properly. The normal percentage of body fat is between 20 and 25 percent of total weight; dancers tend to carry no more than 13 to 18 percent. When the percentage of fat falls below 12 percent, the menstrual cycle is likely to be interrupted. If anorexia is not checked, the body begins to consume itself.

Bulimics indulge in binge eating and purging as a means of controlling their weight. The purging may take the form of induced vomiting, diuretics, or diet pills and laxatives. Extreme damage to teeth, caused by stomach acids, is among the many physical side effects of bulimia.

The National Association of Anorexia Nervosa and Associated Disorders (ANAD), whose headquarters are in Chicago, warns that "early detection and intervention are critical in saving lives. Because many anorexics and bulimics deny that they are ill, family and friends play a critical role in recognizing eating disorder problems and getting help immediately. Although not all victims display all symptoms, several danger signals are commonly associated with anorexia and bulimia."

Symptoms of anorexia nervosa outlined by ANAD:

Deliberate self-starvation with weight loss
Intense, persistent fear of gaining weight
Refusal to eat
Continuous dieting
Denial of hunger
Compulsive exercise
Excessive facial/body hair
Distorted body image
Abnormal weight loss
Sensitivity to cold
Absent or irregular menstruation
Hair loss

Symptoms of bulimia nervosa outlined by ANAD:

Preoccupation with food
Binge eating, usually in secret
Vomiting after binge eating
Abuse of laxatives, diuretics, diet pills, or emetics
Compulsive exercising
Swollen salivary glands
Broken blood vessels in eyes

Telling an anorexic that she is too thin is futile. ANAD suggests there are several things that are better left unsaid to someone who shows signs of an eating disorder and that it's best to shift the focus away from food, weight or appearance. They also emphasize that eating disorders are slow to resolve and patience and professional help may be needed. A dancer with anorexic tendencies may return to a more healthful relationship with food and a more realistic self-image, preoccupation with weight and food may never truly leave them.

Early intervention is essential in breaking the self-destructive cycle. If your child exhibits even one of the symptoms listed above, accompanied by a 10 percent weight loss, treatment should be sought immediately.

Even in the preprofessional dance world, your child will be exposed to extreme opinions about weight management. A realistic self-image, a healthy attitude toward food, and a supportive and loving environment will go a long way in preventing obsessive behavior.

A life in dance demands extraordinary commitment. Dancers work long hours to keep their instrument (the body) in peak condition. Student from the School of Madison Ballet, Madison, Wisconsin. © 2015 Maureen Janson

10

ENTERING THE PROFESSION

THE GREATEST DIFFERENCE AMONG DANCE companies
is size, not idiom. Large companies will be administered in
similar ways, be they modern dance, jazz, or ballet. There
are few companies that do not have a stylistically mixed repertory. The large company may have an extended touring
schedule, although regional companies, such as the Houston
Ballet or the Louisville Ballet, tend to cultivate their hometown audiences.

Small and medium-sized companies, especially modern
dance groups, may supplement their performing schedule
with an outreach program, offering lectures or demonstra-
tions in public schools. Both large and medium-sized companies generally offer a contract for between 22 weeks and
a full year. Additionally, they often have associated schools
that employ their dancers as teachers.

Small companies and "pickup" groups engage dancers
on a freelance basis for a specific series of performances.
They seldom offer contracts; dancers may get paid per performance. But they form the grass roots from which bigger
endeavors may spring.

AUDITIONS

By the time students are ready to audition for their first professional engagement, they will have had, in all likelihood, some experience with the process through an audition for a summer program or a special performance. Whether seeking admission to a university program or membership in a dance company, dancers must always audition, which generally means that the prospective members take a class, submit an audition video, or both.

For a live audition, auditionees should come fully prepared to dance and have all that they need to make a neat and efficient impression, such as a plain leotard and tights, shoes that have been broken in, enough hairpins to keep the hair in place, and a couple of safety pins in case a ribbon or strap comes loose. Sweatpants or bulky legwarmers should never be worn at an audition.

If the audition starts with barre work, the dancer should select a place where she or he will be comfortable. It is best not to stand in corners if the audition is crowded; otherwise legs may get tangled with the person standing at the right angle. Coming into the center, it's best for the dancer not to hang back, but to step to the front of the class. This action will show self-confidence, and will also enable them to be seen clearly. Additionally, it will provide the auditionee with a better view of the teacher demonstrating the combination. If the class is divided into groups, the dancer should not wait for the last group to step forward. By joining the first or second group, the dancer demonstrates that she or he is a quick learner. Similarly, when combinations are given from the corner on a diagonal, the dancer should join one of the first groups going across the floor. It is best to avoid asking questions like "Which arm is up?" or "Do we start with the right leg back?" Instead, the dancer should look closely at all the details demonstrated by the teacher, marking the combination so that it is firmly set in the mind and body. Being aware of the demonstrator's style is especially important in jazz and modern dance auditions; the auditioner will be looking at adaptability.

Some companies request that the dancer supply a resume and photograph at the time of the audition or prior to the audition via email. The fact that the dancer may not have a lot of professional experience should not prove a hindrance. Companies are generally more interested in the kind of training that the dancers have received, their current level of proficiency, and their ability to grasp combinations of choreography. I was once engaged for a film almost solely on the strength of having studied with Olga Preobrazhenskaya. Before we were asked to dance, the director wanted to know where we had studied, and she retained only the people that she felt had received correct training.

Video auditioning has become a common method of dance company member selection process, and it opens the door to greater opportunities for those who are unable to travel for auditions. In many cases, performing arts high school programs that offer a dance concentration will also allow audition via video. Often video is used as a prescreening method after which a dancer might be invited to participate in a live audition or callback.

Since the tools for making a digital video are readily available, it's not difficult to create an acceptable audition. Most companies will outline the expectations for a video but the following, as based on suggestions by *Dance Magazine,* are good general rules of thumb:

An audition video should be between 5–15 minutes in length.

As for live auditions, hair should be secured and tidy, and tight-fitting clothing that clearly shows the line of the body should be worn. Be sure to wear clothing that does not blend in with the floors or walls in which you are filming. And do not wear leg warmers or other baggy clothing.

Although it's not necessary, it is acceptable to speak at the beginning of the video, briefly introducing yourself.

For school auditions, generally it's best to include select barre work exercises, including plié, tendu, rond de jambe, adagio, and grande battement. Centre exercises should include a range, perhaps demonstrating adagio, turns, and small and large jumps.

For a professional audition, it might be expected to highlight a variation or two, and men should include a duet to demonstrate partnering skills.

Always select material carefully according to the styles desired by the company or school. If contemporary styles are part of the audition, plan to show a range and include the dynamics of turns, jumps, floorwork, and dancing at varied speeds.

When filming, it's best to enlist the help of someone to monitor the camera. Make sure the camera, or recording device is steady or on a tripod. The full body of the dancer should be visible at all times. Try some test footage first to make sure the lighting makes the image clear. Remove clutter from the background as much as possible. The best videos do not require much editing, as the editing process can make the audition footage look sloppy. Planning ahead and rehearsing the sequence can save a lot of time and create a seamless and concise audition. Check with the company website for the specifics of submitting the audition video, as parameters vary. Some companies require a DVD submission, while others prefer submissions downloaded electronically through their website. Each company or school has its own requirements.

Live audition formats will also vary. If the audition is for a specific production, like *The Nutcracker,* for which the company simply needs to supplement its roster of dancers, the auditioners will probably be looking for dancers to fill specific parts. If, on the other hand, the audition is held to engage contract dancers for an entire season, the director may be looking for someone to fit into the current repertory. Some companies favor tall dancers; others prefer shorter ones. Some like dancers of a normal weight; others accept only bone-thin dancers. It is wise to inquire, before making a trip to a distant city, what kind of physique the company favors. Modern companies tend to be more open about the physique and engage dancers on the strength of their technique, style, and personality.

Competition is fierce in the dance world, especially for female dancers. There are just too many aspiring ballerinas and not enough good companies to provide employment for all of them. Once a student has been accepted into a company, the competition for advancement is largely a matter of talent and personality. The lucky dancers find their choreographer, or the choreographer finds his or her interpreter. There have been some notable partnerships of this kind. Choreographer Frederick Ashton (1904–1988) had dancer Margot Fonteyn (1919–1991); John Cranko (1927–1973) had Marcia Haydee (b. 1937); Kenneth Macmillan (1929–1992) had Lynn Seymour (b. 1939); and George Balanchine featured a different ballerina in each of the phases of his creative life. Of course, these dancers form an elite circle open to few; countless successful dancers have not found this kind of public recognition but have nevertheless had fulfilling careers.

Despite the competitiveness of the dance world, dancers as a group tend to be supportive of each other. They form within any one company a close community with common goals and common complaints. Because dancers work such long hours, they have little opportunity to form friendships outside the group. This is especially true of companies that have a busy touring schedule. Sometimes dancers do not even know which city they are visiting, unless they have a few free hours during the day and the hosts make a special effort to allow for some sightseeing expeditions. This closeness also breeds a certain exclusivity, whereupon new members may not be welcomed into the inner circle immediately and may find their first weeks in a company somewhat solitary. Perhaps this attitude is no different from that of other workplaces, but it is simply magnified here because the dance company is such a closed environment. Its members are forced to rely on each other to a degree that outsiders find difficult to understand or appreciate.

FINDING WORK

A young dancer can obtain her or his first engagement in various ways. The services of an agent are not necessary unless the dancer seeks commercial work, such as television, films, or industrials (shows that cater to conventions). Most Broadway-type shows hold open auditions, sometimes termed "cattle calls" because they attract so many applicants. These auditions are generally advertised on various casting and job websites. Many regional ballet companies also advertize their needs and audition dates on their own websites and in *Dance Magazine,* among other dance publications. Established modern dance and jazz companies sometimes hold internal auditions for their roster of apprentices. Auditions are usually held in the spring for the following season beginning in September. However, a company will seldom turn away a prospective member if she or he happens to be in town and contacts the organization; the dancer will be invited to take a class, and if there are no immediate vacancies, the dancer will at least be known the next time she or he auditions. Some companies even have a policy of open classes, through which people who are not in the company can take class with company members. Each company is bound to have its own guidelines, and it is a good idea to check them before embarking on a tour of prospects.

Besides the cold-audition route, many dancers find work through personal recommendation. The home teacher may have some contacts, or a visiting guest teacher may be willing to write a recommendation or suggest a venue. Attending a summer workshop may result in an invitation to join the associated company or become an apprentice. An apprenticeship is not a guarantee of acceptance into the company, but it is one step closer.

Some organizations like to imbue the dancers with their particular style, so they insist that dancers undergo a period of apprenticeship or attend their associated school prior to being considered for the company. When auditioning for a first professional engagement the dancer will, in most cases, be engaged initially as an apprentice. The more prestigious the company, the greater choice of dancers the company has, and therefore the more restrictions they place on prospective members.

Like many professions, the dance field is all too easily exploitive. Dancers are often viewed as a commodity—if the dancer does not fulfill the initial promise, a dozen others are waiting in the wings. Dancers need to be aware that they are easily replaceable; but they must also watch for situations that may endanger their health, such as a punishing rehearsal schedule, lack of regular technique classes, or a high turn-over rate. They need to remember that being accepted into a particular company is only the beginning. They must not only maintain their technique but improve it if they want to qualify for better roles; and, above all, their first allegiance must be to their own growth and well-being.

In larger companies, many of the dancers belong to the American Guild of Musical Artists (AGMA) union. A union contract specifies how many hours dancers are expected to rehearse on nonperformance as well as performance days. On a normal day, one without a performance, dancers can rehearse for up to six hours; this is in addition to a company technique class. On a performance day, dancers may only rehearse for two hours. When they are performing twice in a single day, they may not rehearse at all. More than 30 hours per week of rehearsal allows the dancer to earn overtime pay. When on tour, they may travel travel hours are usually regulated, and the number of hours may be limited.

The union contract also specifies wages. The national standard for a first-year dancer's salary per week generally falls within a range based on the size of a company. As an example, a first-year corps dancer at New York City Ballet earns considerably more than a first-year corps dancer in

Tulsa Ballet Theater. The salary rises each year but is also dependent on the artist's ranking or seniority, or both. According to AGMA, fees are not usually based on roles. However, American Ballet Theatre has implemented what they call "step-up pay," which is a small fee for any dancer in the corps de ballet who "steps up" into a soloist or principal role. Any contract may not be for a year but for a specified number of weeks, as few as 22 weeks in some instances. During the layoff period, dancers may accept engagements with other companies, teach, or go on unemployment.

Often, professional dancers who are interested in choreography will branch off and create their own works independently. This format has created many more opportunities for dancers to perform, but represents the other end of the scale; countless small, nonunion companies that may pay little per week or pay the dancers on a per-performance basis. Usually the length of time of the work is brief—it may be just a few performances over one weekend, but it allows dancers to fill in gaps in employment elsewhere, and to maintain performance conditioning, which is sometimes quite difficult when off-time is extended. If there is a contract, it usually covers a relatively short span of time. Dancers employed by these small companies usually have to supplement their incomes with part-time jobs.

Even within the realm of dance performance, careers are possible beyond the stage, via television and Internet. Opportunities with small dance companies, corporate events, and independent choreographers create demand for more professional dancers. Early music videos paved the way for performing on television, with MTV bringing dance to mainstream television in the early 1980s. This has led to video platforms such as YouTube and Vimeo, which have become a place to broadcast dance freely. Television shows such as *Dancing with the Stars* and *So You Think You Can Dance* have placed previously unknown ballet and modern dancers in the spotlight, and have brought dance to living rooms around the globe, further expanding opportunities in the profession.

TOURING

A professional dancer must be prepared to work when others rest (evenings and holidays) as well as when others work (morning classes, afternoon rehearsals, or daytime performances). A dancer will also be away from home a great deal. Few dance companies can survive by performing solely in their home city, so touring is an integral part of the season.

Touring may be anything from short day or overnight trips to weeks on the road. Generally, the sole responsibility of dancers is to be at the departure point on time; travel and accommodations are arranged by the company. Some companies turn over to the dancers the frequent-flyer mileage accumulated during the tour, which sometimes provides for a vacation trip during the off-season. However, the dancers are responsible for their personal effects and for taking care of their laundry needs. Sometimes they even have to wash their own costumes, and are then given extra money to cover the cost. While on tour with a larger company, dancers often receive a per diem allowance toward meals. The allowance varies according to the cost of living in the city or country visited. Some companies give a higher allowance when the hotel bill is the responsibility of the dancer.

Eating while on tour may present a challenge. Many smaller cities do not have restaurants that stay open late at night, and finding a place to eat after a performance may pose a challenge. Winifred Haun, who toured as a member of Joseph Holmes Chicago Dance Theatre for eight years, says that people tend to either lose or gain weight during the touring season. Often the only available food is from fast-food restaurants, and finding the type of food you usually eat is difficult. She adds, however, that sometimes presenters will provide refreshments after a performance; "small amenities really make us happy."

Patty Eylar, a former member of the Chicago Ballet, says that it is too easy to get out of shape on tour: "We have classes on performance days, but not on the days when we are traveling. It is hard to find studios that will give you a space for class. The stage manager finds restaurants for us or picks up sandwiches for the company. We do laundry on our day off. It's hard." She speaks of touring in Europe as having been especially difficult: "Every time we wanted to eat, the stores were closed. Everyone was taking a nap!" On one occasion, traveling from France to Italy, the road was closed, the bus had to take a detour, and the dancers ended up being on the road for 21 hours. But "we saw some wonderful scenery."

While the novelty of touring may be exciting at the beginning, dancers soon miss their habitual surroundings. Haun says, "You find that you are thrown in the company of people that you would not generally have much in common with." Whenever we find ourselves in new surroundings with irregular routines, we tend to lose the anchoring that a regular routine provides. To maintain healthy eating habits, a degree of technique, and a sense of humor takes a lot of discipline.

A life in dance demands extraordinary commitment. Dancers work long hours at a physically exhausting task. They need to keep their instrument (the body) in peak condition despite the wear and tear of travel. As Ivan Nagy commented on the disparity of the perceived glamour of the profession and its reality, "You do a plié in New York, or London, or Moscow, and it still hurts." Dancers lead, for the most part, an existence that is somewhat isolated from the mainstream—often the busiest season for a company is vacation time for the rest of society. For most dancers, dance is not what they do but who they are. Dancing could be likened to climbing a mountain. As you take each step, you exult in your ability to do so, your muscles hurt, your hands (or feet) bleed, you labor to reach the next plateau, and, looking upward, you see how far you have yet to scale. And there is joy in looking at the road yet to be traveled, because the joy is in the doing.

With the hardships that a life in dance implies, dancers are extremely lucky people, engaged in doing what they love. The discipline of dance provides transcendent moments on a daily basis. Our culture is given to finding "last frontiers" to fuel the imagination: the West, Alaska, outer space. Dancers are actively engaged in conquering their frontier every day; aching muscles and less than ideal working conditions are a small price to pay for the privilege.

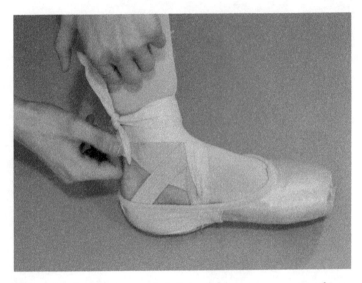

Ultimately, a legitimate career in ballet and dance can mean many things. Secondary education is often the place where a dancer can learn about and experience these possibilities and gain a well-rounded experience. Student from the School of Madison Ballet, Madison, Wisconsin. © 2015 Maureen Janson

11

SECONDARY EDUCATION

AND BEYOND

MODERN DANCE WAS THE TECHNIQUE that led the way for dance to become a discipline taught at the college level. The first university dance major program in the United States was actually started by a nondancer, Margaret H'Doubler at the University of Wisconsin in 1926. Initially hired to coach basketball, H'Doubler's early teachings stressed dance as expression and communication rather than as an art form. A few years later, Bennington College in Vermont held its first summer dance course in 1934 and soon became a mecca for many dancers who wanted to work with the modern dance pioneers who taught at the college—people like Martha Graham, Hanya Holm, Doris Humphrey, and Charles Weidman.

After World War II university dance programs proliferated, but ballet was not incorporated into higher education curricula on any appreciable scale until the late 1960s. Today hundreds of colleges and universities offer a dance degree while countless others provide dance courses as some part of their general curriculum. Ballet and modern dance are usually, but not always, taught side by side within the same program, and dance departments are often staffed by current and former professional dancers.

ABOUT COLLEGE PROGRAMS

Your involvement as a parent in your child's dance training is likely to continue when the dancer attends college. If he or she chooses to study in an academic setting, some homework is advisable, as selecting a school and embarking on dance degree in college is a significant financial and time commitment. One university program may seem much the same as another on the surface, yet a deeper look can determine a program's particular strengths and help to match them with personal interests.

In an undergraduate college dance major program, besides general education subjects and dance technique courses in ballet and modern dance, students can expect to learn kinesiology, somatics (Pilates, yoga or body awareness, and conditioning techniques), dance history, dance theory, cultural dance forms, and the basic principles of choreography. As opportunities in the field expand, some programs also offer courses (and occasionally major or minor studies) in topics such as dance writing and criticism, video and screendance, arts management, injury prevention and dance medicine, and movement science.

Studying up on the faculty and teaching staff of a particular program will lend a greater understanding to the style of that program. Reading biographical information on the dance faculty website provides insight into the stylistic focus of a program. For example, the current chair of the ballet department at Indiana University comes from

Royal Ballet School training, while Distinguished Professor Violette Verdy brings a Balanchine-influenced experience to the faculty there. The training will be eclectic, as in most programs, but the student here has access to both the British and Balanchine styles.

Most dance programs include an active performing schedule, but again they vary greatly in both content and quality depending on the interests and backgrounds of the faculty. In some departments modern dance is emphasized, while in others ballet predominates. More and more often college programs have affiliations with a local ballet or modern dance company, providing a further outlet for the students to gain performance experience and make professional connections.

College programs are not without their flaws, and can be a breeding atmosphere for competition. Often very rigorous scheduling demands that students dance for up to eight or more hours a day, while expected to carry a traditional academic load as well. Injuries, mental and emotional stress, and fatigue can be the side effects of such demands. Eating disorders still frequently surface among college dancers, and undergraduate years can make or break the professional. Awareness of these dangers can help a teen dancer prepare to make the leap to college and in turn to a career in dance.

The knowledge gained during a four-year undergraduate program usually outweighs the challenges. College studies enhance the physical experience of dance and enable the dancer to develop into a knowledgeable and articulate teacher or choreographer. Far from being a detraction, those years allow the individual to grow, form opinions, and develop into an artist with a full grasp of the chosen art form. Doors open, and dancers become aware of peripheral opportunities in the field. Additional benefits of a college education are the contacts that students make through the resident faculty and visiting artists. These contacts provide entry both into the professional world and into teaching, choreography, or administration. Additionally, earning the undergraduate degree makes the transition to another career easier when the performing years are over.

Moreover, while most modern dance companies unquestionably prefer their dancers to have reached a certain level of maturity, many ballet companies are also turning to more mature, well-rounded dancers. They appreciate the deeper understanding of motion and emotion that seasoned performers bring to the repertory.

Every year *Dance Magazine* publishes a comprehensive guide to universities and colleges. Additionally, many universities hold national auditions and advertise the dates and locations in this popular magazine. A dance student who wishes to enter a college dance program should initiate some investigation a year or two ahead of the entry year. This time will allow for some visits and observations that will help in the selection of a program best suited to the student's talents and interests.

Keep in mind that secondary education need not be focused solely on training for performance. The presence of technology coupled with the growing recognition of the importance of an arts training as providing beneficial education for all careers, have broadened the higher education model for dance. As mentioned, one might study to become a dance historian, a dance filmmaker, or a dance writer.

Secondary education is often the place where a dancer can learn about and experience these possibilities and gain a well-rounded experience. Ultimately, a legitimate career in ballet and dance can mean many things. If the dancer does not have the technical prowess and chops to aim for performance work with a large-scale company, that should not put college studies out of the realm of possibility.

A DANCING CAREER

A commonly held belief in dance is that younger is not only better: it is essential. According to some dance professionals, if one is intent on a dance career, the years spent attending college are dangerously detracting. But as we now know, a college education has many benefits, although it may not be the choice of all dancers on a professional career track.

Many young dancers feel compelled to enter professional dance schools or apprenticeship within a company often without even having finished high school. Some professionals hold that those who have not achieved the status of soloist by the age of 21 or 22 will, in all probability, never rise beyond the ranks of the corps de ballet. In order to become a soloist, one must be dancing professionally by the age of 18 at the latest. In other words, all energies, leading up to acceptance into a company, must be directed toward dancing; there can be no question of a college education interrupting the momentum.

While the late teens are unquestionably essential formative years during which young dancers must be engaged in honing their skills, this denies a young dancer the chance to enjoy other regular teenage experiences and ignores the many alternatives that are available for continuing an education. These alternatives include enrolling as a part-time student in a university while engaged in a professional company.

The above model for a dancing career is based on the European and Russian ballet schools, where children enter a professional school at the age of nine or ten and are educated within the institution. Alexandre Demidov writes, in his *Russian Ballet Past and Present*, "The training in ballet schools is aimed not only at developing professional skills but at fostering the general cultural growth of the students who have chosen the hard work of a dancer . . . The curricula of these schools are such that the future ballet dancer will be a broadly educated person, a cultured person in the highest sense of that word" (p. 13). As this statement indicates, the general education of these dancers is not sacrificed to dance. On the contrary, dancers receive a broad, liberal arts education prior to their entry into the professional world; an education, moreover, that bears more resemblance to an undergraduate college program than it does to the standards of most American high schools.

The performing life within dance is relatively short. By age 35, if not sooner, dancers begin to think of alternate ways to make a living. Furthermore, the risk of injury is always present. The emotional impact of an injury is compounded by the fear that you may be overlooked for roles. Claire Bataille, former principal dancer with Hubbard Street Dance Chicago, comments, "You dance when injured because you are afraid they may forget about you." The greatest fear of all may be that of not being able to dance anymore. But what kind of choices, for example, does a 29-year-old dancer have, when she or he does not even have a high school diploma and has never done anything but dance since the age of eight? The very brevity of this career supports the argument for a college education.

One of the purposes of education is surely to provide choices. A dancer's education is often lopsided. Concentrating from an early age on this physically demanding activity may lead to neglecting other aspects of development. Higher education opens up opportunities unimaginable to a 14-year-old whose horizons are bounded by the ballet studio. The four years spent at a college or university may prove the very stepping stone one needs for a successful and rewarding career. Not only will they provide the benefits of the intellectual pursuits that are the fabric of education, but they also may open doors to the professional dance world through the friendships formed and the artists met. The experience of a college education may also, later on, facilitate the transition away from a dancing career. It may suggest exciting choices and help the dancer assess her or his strengths and interests.

BEYOND PERFORMING

Many dance-related careers are open to dancers. Some require an undergraduate college degree, while others may warrant either further college education or on-the-job-training.

Teaching

The most obvious career choice for continuing a direct association with dance is teaching. The only real requirement for teaching at a studio is a thorough knowledge of the art form.

While a college degree is not required to open a dance studio, a knowledge of business will help the studio be financially successful. Dance teachers face landlords and leases and must keep accurate records, balance expenses against income, and pay taxes. They must also know how to advertise their program and how to devise a curriculum and often the studio owner is working without support staff.

Unless the school will be in a town where there are no other dance schools, teachers need to survey the competition to determine how their proposed program differs from the others and how it will enhance the dance education in that area. This survey will initially help in targeting prospective students and designing a marketing plan to reach them. The best kind of publicity for a new school, however, is both an excellent website and the use of social media. This gives a teacher the opportunity to describe her or his approach and background, and post photos of the studio, students, and faculty. This wide coverage greatly facilitates recruitment.

Devising a curriculum requires knowledge of the developmental aspects of the technique—what is appropriate at various levels and for specific age groups, from creative movement to advanced levels. Neophyte teachers need not rely on their training experience alone to guide them; teacher training courses at a local college are invaluable. Working with a mentor who is knowledgeable about the developmental aspects of dance training is another option. There are also numerous publications on the subject of teaching dance.

If the studio owner does not teach all the classes, there must be a basis for evaluating the competence of those who teach. The same concerns that guide one's own teaching apply to employees—are the material and the pace of the class appropriate? Are the corrections given to students based upon sound principles? Can the teacher demonstrate the motions with competence? The employer may even have to train teachers to conform to her or his ideals.

Rather than assuming the responsibility of opening their own studio, many dancers choose the path of a freelance teacher working in several different studios. Dancers who move on to a freelance teaching career generally choose to remain in the city where they are known through their work with the local dance company. The first step is contacting the local dance schools to make them aware of one's availability. The chief requirement is adaptability; each studio will have its own code of conduct and expectations, and a freelance teacher will have to conform to them.

There are other issues to consider when planning a freelance teaching career. A freelance dance teacher is paid by the class, so one will need to line up enough classes, often in different studios, to make a decent living. The very real drawback to freelancing is the fact that studios generally do not offer health plans or benefits, and there is absolutely no job security: the contracts are often verbal, and classes may be canceled with little notice.

While some university dance programs are headed by former dancers without degrees, these dancers have usually held prominent places in the dance world prior to their retirement into teaching. These same universities require at least a master's degree of their prospective teachers if they have not achieved preeminent status in the professional world. Although many colleges employ dancers without degrees in adjunct faculty positions, the dancer must hold at least a master's degree to be eligible for tenure track positions.

Adjunct faculty depend upon yearly contracts and, like freelance teachers, have no benefits. Salaries for adjuncts are usually quite low, so adjuncts often find it necessary to supplement income by teaching at other places.

With a bachelor's degree, reentry and completion of a master's degree in a university graduate program is usually fairly straightforward. Even if not, the prospect of several years spent obtaining these two degrees should not be daunting. Colleges often give credit for life experience and for competency in one's field. Additionally, there are some master's degree programs, such as the graduate program at the University of Wisconsin-Milwaukee, that now offer special situations to returning professionals, allowing them to keep up with a performing and touring schedule while attending credit courses over the summers.

Teaching dance at public middle and high schools is also an option. However, state certification is generally required for eligibility. Different states have different criteria; some require certification prior to employment, while others allow the dance teacher to obtain certification while teaching.

Choreography

It has been said that choreographers are not made but born, that dancers cannot learn choreography but must be blessed with some innate talent. There are, however, many levels of choreographic endeavors. All teachers are choreographers, because designing a class involves combining steps in interesting ways. Composing for a class, however, differs from composing a ballet. A teacher is bound by the rules of the technique, whereas choreographers, like poets, can break academic rules to achieve desired effects. Choreographers need a sense of composition (an eye for patterns and balance in space); musicality (an ear not only for the rhythmic patterns but also for the emotional content of a musical composition); an ability to abstract feelings and translate them into motion; and the ability to tell a story using motion instead of words. Working with young children also requires adaptability, a tempering of what one imagines to the technical and emotional level of the students.

These qualities can be developed through association with and participation in the repertory of a company. Great choreographers of the past, such as Marius Petipa, Mikhail Fokine, Frederick Ashton, Antony Tudor, and George Balanchine, learned the craft of choreography in this manner. Not only did they have a strong desire to create dances, but they were given the opportunity to refine their craft over a long period of time. They learned through trial and error; they experienced failures as well as outstanding successes.

Experimenting with choreography is a little more difficult logistically than, for example, painting a picture, A painter needs a canvas and paints, but choreographers need trained bodies and minds who are capable of interpreting their ideas. A dance does not exist before it is danced. Choreography involves long hours in the studio exploring possibilities, testing ideas, refining sequences, throwing out sections that do not work, and beginning again. It is a very public act of creation. No one knows how long a writer sat in front of a blank computer screen or empty notebook before a paragraph was written; choreographers do not have that luxury. They must create within the framework of rehearsal schedules and performance dates, relying on the energy and talent of their dancers to do justice to their vision.

When the opportunity to see and take part in an outstanding repertory is limited, or missing altogether, the rules of the craft can be learned. Colleges offer courses in choreography in which its tenets can be explored. Artistically, composing a dance is very much like composing a picture. The painter uses line, texture, and color; the choreographer uses line, motion, and dynamics. The intent of both is the same—to create a composition that will please, move, or stimulate the viewer and challenge the dancer.

Choreographic experimentation is costly. Ballet company directors are often reluctant to entrust an inexperienced choreographer with the production of a ballet, primarily because of the commitment of the dancers' time and energy. They also hesitate to cover all the adjunct costs of costuming and mounting the new production. Modern dance choreographers fare no better, and often create their own opportunities to show their work. There are, however, state and federal grants that can help a young choreographer produce a concert. An Internet search can reveal national and local grant opportunities.

If a dancer is driven to be a choreographer, she or he should take every opportunity to make dances, keep a quality video record of achievements, and choose venues where works will be seen, like the regional companies' festivals, or associate with other choreographers with the same goals.

Writing: History, Research, and Criticism

Writing about dance is a very rewarding option for former dancers, but one that requires an academic as well as a dancing background. Many dance critics, historians, and researchers writing today were originally dancers. However, the critic needs to have some education in writing, preferably either English or journalism courses. Many dance critics start out writing reviews for their university publication. Others gain early experience by creating their own blog and thus their own opportunity to write and publish their work.

The critic needs a wide knowledge of the dance repertory to write a good review, one that will not only describe the dance but place it in its historical context. I remember reading a review of *Cakewalk,* a ballet by Ruthanna Boris (1918–2007), in which Boris parodies ballets from different periods of history. The reviewer missed the references altogether, and thereby missed the opportunity to enlighten and educate the public.

If a dancer has an aptitude for writing, an ability to see and describe motion as well as intent and hidden meanings, dance criticism may well be an option to pursue. An increase in number of blogs hosting dance criticism has opened options in the field.

History and research are two fields that depend almost exclusively on an university affiliation. Writing dance books is not a lucrative profession (unless you write bestsellers); almost everyone in the field holds a teaching position. Research often demands a great deal of time and expenditure and is not readily available to people who are not affiliated with a university. Although grants are available to people who can present a good rationale for their interest in a particular area, these awards are most readily accessible to university professors.

Administration and Arts Management

Arts management has become a viable venue for former dancers because it requires a thorough knowledge of the arts world. However, the field is highly specialized and requires specific courses at a university or college. The responsibilities of the managing director of a dance company may include: staff and facility management; grant preparation and administration; budget development and oversight; negotiation of artists' contracts; and marketing. The managing director must also work closely with the artistic director in the strategic planning of the performance schedule. If a dancer is organized, has a good presence, and can juggle a variety of tasks—setting a touring schedule, talking to prospective donors, balancing a budget, and understanding the dynamics of a repertory—then, with training, she or he will probably be able to rise to the challenge of managing a dance company.

Therapy Modalities

Numerous schools offer training in massage therapy. Dancers make good massage therapists because they already have an appreciation of muscular functions, have great anatomical awareness and probably possess firsthand experience with the specific problems caused by pulled muscles, strains, sprains, and body aches. The training period for professional massage is of short duration. A year or two of intensive study will usually provide the skills necessary to become a massage therapist.

Dance/movement therapy, on the other hand, requires a background in psychology. Goucher College in Maryland, Hunter College in New York, UCLA, University of Wisconsin-Madison, and Columbia College in Chicago, among others, offer excellent certification programs in dance/movement therapy. This growing field has much to offer to people who are interested in extending their dance knowledge into a fascinating area of healing.

Production, Lighting, and Design

Theatrical technical production includes many specialties, but most people in this field have a background in visual

arts and design. Many universities offer production programs that provide an opportunity for hands-on experience
in designing, mounting, and running a show. A dance background can be a stepping stone, as it provides an appreciation for specific dance concerns in both lighting and costume
designing.

Video, Screendance, and Television

If one wishes to enter the media world from the dance world,
the primary interest will probably be in filming and editing
dance. A fascinating field, filming can range from straightforward documentation (putting a dance on video in order
to facilitate later reconstructions) to artistic collaborations
between a choreographer and a video artist, in which the
camera or the editing process is used as a means of expression.

Again, the technical aspects of the profession can be
learned in both colleges and professional schools such as the
University of Utah, which offers a certificate program specifically in screendance. Dancers entering this field bring to it their
own particular vision, honed by years of exploring motion.

Former dancers can be found in a variety of other professions: the law, anthropology, psychiatry, physical therapy,
medicine, theatre production, and acting. Although dancers may feel that they are ill-prepared for any other work,
dance training instills a highly developed sense of discipline
that helps the artists achieve success in whatever field they
choose.

A young ballet student faces a challenging yet rewarding road ahead. Student from the School of Madison Ballet, Madison, Wisconsin. ©2015 Maureen Janson

12

PARENTING THE DANCER

WE ARE ALWAYS A LITTLE surprised and somewhat delighted when our children show a dedication and a commitment that seems to us beyond their years. Parenting a dancer is not very different from parenting any talented child.

Children generally begin dance classes at an early age, when dance is, in many cases, an activity chosen by their parents. Sometimes the children identify their desire, which can have a healthy, maturing effect. One mother commented to me, "It is a fascinating experience to be led by your child. It opened our lives. We do a lot of things that we would not have done, like going to dance concerts." Usually between the ages of nine and 12, children begin to let their preference be known. Either the parent continues to drag the reluctant child to dance class for a few more years, or dance assumes a central position in the child's life.

Parents readily admit that parenting a dancing child is very demanding. One parent says, "If the child is committed, you must be committed too." This commitment begins with driving the child to and from class. "It takes a lot of time," another parent said. "There was a studio nearby, but it was not very good, so I drove her into town every day until she was sixteen and could drive." This mother admitted that she could not exercise much control over her daughter; "this was something that she wanted to do, and we tried to support and encourage her."

Parents must be prepared to help their child cope with rejection. Dancers need a loving environment, because they may not get enough emotional support from their dance teacher, and often the dance teacher assumes a central role in shaping their self-image. If there are too many students in a class, or if the teacher is indifferent, the child will suffer. Another mother explained to me that she had taken her daughter out of the leading studio in her city because "the classes were too big, the students had little individual attention, and my daughter's self-esteem was suffering from the neglect." On the other hand, if the teacher is supportive and encouraging, the child will gain the confidence to thrive in class. The mother of two dancing daughters commented, "We have not pushed them, but just helped them pursue what they want—gave them options, helped them stay motivated."

Making sure that their dancers eat the right food is another concern voiced by parents. Some children are very conscientious about their diet, but most need guidance. The mother of the two daughters said, "We have become more aware because of their needs. Our diet has more vegetables and protein in it, and very little fat. It is often a challenge to squeeze meals into the daily class schedule."

A young and dedicated dancer soon has to make some hard choices. Her or his social time is greatly curtailed, if not totally eliminated. One mother lamented, "When she was 13, all her friends deserted her. She started sobbing, then realized that she could not have it all." This mother was very upset, but she knew that she could not help. She had to let her daughter sort out her priorities. This experience had a maturing effect; the child became more self-reliant as her determination to become a dancer grew.

Most parents I have spoken to are acutely aware of the dangers of becoming a stage parent. "As a parent, you have to step back, not let your dreams get mixed up with the child's; not impose yours on hers. It has to be what she wants." When the child's motivation is not clear, there is always the danger that she or he will become a "pleaser." When this happens, a part of the personality is lost. Dancers then tend to see their worth only in terms of what other people think of them.

Symbiotic relationships are not uncommon between dancers and their mothers. These can be positive when the desires of the child concur with those of the mother, and there have been some legendary mother/daughter relationships. Tamara Toumanova (1919–1996), one of Balanchine's baby ballerinas, was always accompanied by her mother; they were totally devoted to each other. Violette Verdy, was also devoted to her mother, who not only looked after Verdy's needs but mothered every member of the company. But these relationships can also have a dark side. One of the summer students at a school where I was once teaching had come from another state with her mother. Back home, the mother was working at the dance studio that the child attended. The mother watched every class and was always waiting with comments and corrections when her daughter came out of class. If you offered a cookie, the mother would say, "We're on a diet." She also stated, on one occasion, "We are allergic to milk" and, "We go to bed early." The child was mostly silent, smiling, and compliant. The mother was making plans to move to the city to provide her daughter with the opportunity to study further with her summer teachers. Sometime later I received a letter from the mother: the child had broken her ankle, and they had returned to their hometown. The mother spoke of the injury as a terrible accident, but maybe this was the only way the daughter could make her wishes known to her domineering parent.

There is a fine line between support and coercion. The decision to become a dancer may be made at a tender age; the aspiring dancer hardly out of childhood when committing to a way of life that she or he barely apprehends. That life is too hard to be imposed from the outside. Well-wishing parents who may be fulfilling their own unrealized dreams are unwittingly setting the scene for a disaster. Not only will their own dreams be dashed, but the child will suffer from a sense of guilt when she or he fails to achieve the dream for them both. The child's only recourse is often a dramatic, usually unconscious gesture that will free her or him of the situation and the guilt. Dance parents generally tend to be highly involved in their children's lives. Certainly the time they commit to the activity of dance is considerable. As the student progresses through the technique, she or he must spend more and more time on it. It is often hard for the parent to maintain a healthy distance under these circumstances. But it is essential for parents to be able to distinguish between their hopes and aspirations and those of their child; they must provide the child enough room to mature and define her or his own goals.

Parents must also be prepared to make a financial commitment. Paying for classes and keeping the dancer supplied with shoes can strain a budget. Dance class is not a luxury; it is the very breath of the dancer. Without class, technique cannot be maintained and progress cannot be made. If your child is talented, most schools will provide a scholarship at best, a lower tuition rate at least. Never hesitate to ask about financial assistance. The most important thing is for your child's training to go on uninterrupted.

Remember that dance is more than a job; it is a way of life, whether you have strong misgivings about your child pursuing a career in dance or you totally support this choice. To paraphrase Martha Graham, if one has been chosen by having been given certain attributes and longings, one must honor the gift.

Mary Wigman's wise words in *The Language of Dance* (1966) are a fitting conclusion:

> Certainly we are able to do a great deal when it comes to molding and forming, to furthering and developing. But it is not in our power to create the often hotly desired talent. We are not even able to determine the degree and kind of talent. For if nature has not planted the fuel of artistic talent in man, no power, no desire, no will is able to ignite the torch to that flaming light in which the creative force can give of itself lavishly, in which the language of dance finds its heightened expression in a work of art and the dancer becomes the carrier and messenger of the art of dancing. Talent is a blessing. And so is the pedagogic talent in dance. Our task, however, lies in serving: to serve the dance, to serve the work, to serve man, and to serve life.

APPENDIX

High Schools for the Arts

Aces Educational Center for the Arts (public, magnet)
55 Audubon Street
New Haven, Connecticut 06510
203-777-5451
Disciplines: ballet, modern dance, jazz, tap
Others, by semester: West African, Haitian
www.aces.org/schools-programs/magnet-schools/educational-center-for-the-arts

Douglas Anderson School for the Arts (public)
2445 San Diego Road
Jacksonville, Florida 32207
904-346-5608
Disciplines: ballet, modern dance, jazz, tap, ethnic dance, character dance
Electives: ballet variations, choreography, dance production, men's class www.duvalschools.org/anderson

The Bolles School (private)
7400 San Jose Boulevard
Jacksonville, Florida 32217

Disciplines: ballet, modern dance, jazz, tap, musical theatre, nutrition, dance history, injury prevention, choreography, kinesiology, lighting design
www.bolles.org

Booker T. Washington Magnet High School (public)
2001 West Fairview Avenue
Montgomery, Alabama 36108
334-268-3813
Disciplines: ballet, modern dance, jazz, tap, ethnic, pointe, choreography
www.btw.mps-al.org

Booker T. Washington School for the Performing and Visual Arts (public)
2501 Flora Street
Dallas, Texas 75201
214-720-7300
Disciplines: ballet, modern dance
Electives: jazz, tap, musical theatre, dance history, composition, Labanotation, www.dallasisd.org/bookert

Cab Calloway School of the Arts (public)
100 N. Dupont Road
Wilmington, Delaware 19807
302-651-2702
Disciplines: movement according to students' needs
www.cabcallowayschool.org

George Washington Carver Center for Arts and Technology (public)
938 York Road
Baltimore, Maryland 21204
410-887-2775
Disciplines: ballet, modern dance, Labanotation, composition, modern repertory, dance history
http://carverhs.bcps.org

Carver Creative and Performing Arts Center (magnet)
2001 W. Fairview Avenue
Montgomery, Alabama 36108
334-269-3813

Disciplines: ballet, modern dance, jazz
www.carversr.mps-al.org/

Cass Technical High School (public)
2421 Second Avenue
Detroit, Michigan 48201
313-596-3900
Disciplines: ballet, modern dance (Graham and Horton), jazz, cultural dance, tap, choreography
http://casstech.schools.detroitk12.org

Gibbs High School
Pinellas Country Center for the Arts (magnet)
850 34th Street South
St. Petersburg, Florida 33711
813-893-5452
Disciplines: ballet, modern dance, jazz, tap, character, dance history, kinesiology, cultural
www.pcsb.org/Page/13559

Chicago Academy for the Arts (private)
1010 W. Chicago Avenue
Chicago, IL 60622
312-421-0202
Disciplines: ballet, modern dance (Graham), jazz, pointe/variations, men's class, dance history, kinesiology, body conditioning, dance survey
www.chicagoartsacademy.org

Cooperative Arts & Humanities High School (public)
444 Orange Street
New Haven, Connecticut 06511
203-946-5923
Disciplines: ballet, modern dance, jazz, tap, dance foundations
http://co-opartsandhumanities.org

Denver School of the Arts (public)
7111 Montview Boulevard
Denver, CO 80220
720-424-1700
Disciplines: ballet, modern dance, jazz, tap
http://dsa.dpsk12.org

Duke Ellington High School for the Arts (public)
3500 R Street NW
Washington, DC 20007
202-282-0123
Disciplines: ballet, modern, dance history, improvisation, composition www.ellingtonschool.org

Ralph Waldo Emerson Visual & Performing Arts (public)
716 East 7th Avenue
Gary, Indiana 46402
219-886-6555
Disciplines: ballet, modern dance, jazz, tap, pointe, African dance, choreography
www.garycsc.k12.in.us/schools/william-a-wirt-emerson-vpa/

John L. Le Flore High School of Communication and Arts (magnet)
700 Donald Street
Mobile, Alabama 36617
Disciplines: ballet, modern dance, jazz, tap
http://leflore.mcs.schoolinsites.com

Fine Arts Center (public)
1613 W. Washington Street
Greenville, South Carolina 29601
Disciplines: ballet, modern dance
www.fineartscenter.net

The Governor's School for the Arts (public)
Old Dominion University
Norfolk, Virginia 23529
Disciplines: ballet, modern dance, jazz, tap, ethnic dance, Pilates, pas de deux, dance history, anatomy and kinesiology, rhythmic analysis, Labanotation, movement analysis, improvisation, pointe, variations, repertory
www.gsarts.org

Greater Hartford Academy of the Arts (public, magnet)
15 Vernon Street
Hartford, Connecticut 06106

860-757- 6300
Disciplines: ballet, modern dance, dance history, composition, improvisation, repertory
Electives: tap, jazz, cultural
www.crecschools.org/our-schools/greater-hartford-academy-of-the-arts

La Guardia High School of the Arts (public)
100 Amsterdam Avenue
New York, New York 10023
212-496-0700
Disciplines: ballet, modern dance, survival skills, dance history, acting for dancers, choreography, career management, character, jazz, dance history, tap
http://laguardiahs.org

High School for the Performing & Visual Arts (public)
4001 Stanford Street
Houston, Texas 77006
713-942-1960
Disciplines: ballet, modern dance, jazz, tap, musical theatre, dance history, improvisation, composition, dance photography
www.houstonisd.org/hspvarts

Holland Hall School (public)
5666E 81st Street
Tulsa, Oklahoma 74137
918-481-1111
Disciplines: modern dance (Graham, Limón)
www.hollandhall.org

Idyllwild School of Music and the Arts (private)
P.O. Box 38
Idyllwild, California 92549
909-659-2171
Disciplines: ballet, modern dance, jazz, character, tap, composition, anatomy/kinesiology, dance history, music for dancers, men's class in ballet, modern, jazz
www.idyllwildarts.org

Interlochen Arts Academy (private)
P.O. Box 199
Interlochen, Michigan 49643
616-276-7472
Disciplines: ballet, pointe, character, variations, men's class, part-nering, modern, jazz, improvisation, composition
www.interlochen.org

Los Angeles County High School for the Arts (public)
5151 State University Drive
Los Angeles, CA 90032
323-343-2550
Disciplines: ballet, modern (Horton, Dunham), hip-hop, jazz, composition
www.lachsa.net

Martin Luther King Jr., High School (public)
3200 E. Lafayette
Detroit, Michigan 48207
Disciplines: modern
http://detroit.k12.mi.us/schools/king/

Milwaukee High School of the Arts (public)
2300 W. Highland Avenue
Milwaukee, Wisconsin 53233
414-933-1500
Disciplines: ballet, modern dance, jazz, tap, African dance, choreography
http://milwaukeehighschoolofthearts.org

New Orleans Center for Creative Arts (public)
6048 Perrier Street
New Orleans, Louisiana 70118
504-899-0055
Disciplines: ballet, modern dance, jazz, character, dance history
www.nocca.com

New Trier High School (public)
385 Winnetka Avenue
Winnetka, Illinois 60093
847-446-7000

Disciplines: modern dance, improvisation, composition
www.newtrier.k12.il.us

New World School of the Arts (public)
300 NE 2nd Avenue
Miami, Florida 33132
305-237-3341
Disciplines: ballet, modern dance, jazz, Spanish dance, African
dance, tap, composition, improvisation, dance history, anat-
omy/kinesiology, injury prevention, dance production, dance
criticism, body alignment, performance
http://nwsa.mdc.edu

The New Schools of Carver: School of the Arts (public)
55 McDonough Boulevard
Atlanta, GA 30315
Phone: (404) 802-4415
Disciplines: ballet, modern dance, jazz
www.atlanta.k12.ga.us/Domain/2830

Padua Academy (private, Catholic, girls only)
905 N. Broom Street
Wilmington, Delaware 19806
Disciplines: ballet, tap, jazz
www.paduaacademy.org

Parkview Magnet High School (public)
2501 Barrow Road
Little Rock, Arkansas 72204
501-228-3000
Disciplines: ballet, modern dance, jazz, composition, dance history,
dance ensemble
http://parkview.lrsd3.org/parkview.htm

Pinellas County Center for the Arts at Gibbs School (public)
850 34th Street South
St. Petersburg, Florida 33711
Disciplines: ballet (Vaganova), modern dance (Horton), ethnic,
music for dancers, anatomy and injury prevention, stagecraft,
dance history
www.pccagibbs.com

Dr. Phillips High School, Visual and Performing Arts Magnet (public, preprofessional college prep)
6500 Turkey Lake Road
Orlando, Florida 32819
Disciplines: ballet, modern dance, jazz, pointe, improvisation, dance criticism, dance theory, health and wellness
http://dpdancemagnet.ocps.net/Welcome.html

Pittsburgh High School for the Creative and Performing Arts (public)
925 Brushton Avenue
Pittsburgh, Pennsylvania 15208
412-247-7860
Disciplines: ballet, modern dance, jazz, tap, dance history, anatomy/ physiology
http://discoverpps.org/school.php?id=304

Ruth Asawa San Francisco School of the Arts (public)
700 Font Boulevard
San Francisco, California 94132
415-469-4027
Disciplines: ballet, modern dance, folk, Afro-Asian dance
www.sfsota.org

School for Creative and Performing Arts (public)
1310 Sycamore Street
Cincinnati, Ohio 45210
513-632-5912
Disciplines: ballet, pointe, partnering, character, modern dance (Graham)
www.scpak12.org

University of North Carolina School of the Arts (public)
1533 South Main Street
Winston-Salem, North Carolina 27127-2738
336-770-3399
Disciplines: ballet, contemporary
www.uncsa.edu/

Walnut Hill School (private)
12 Highland Street
Natick, Massachussets 01760
508-650-5020
Disciplines: ballet, pointe
http://walnuthillarts.org

Youth Performing Arts School (public)
1517 South Second Street
Louisville, Kentucky 40208
502-485-8355
Disciplines: ballet, modern dance, jazz
www.jefferson.k12.ky.us/Schools/Special/ypas.html

In Canada

Canterbury High School (magnet)
900 Canterbury Avenue
Ottawa, Ontario K1G 3A7
613-731-1191
Disciplines: ballet, modern dance, composition, theory, history
www.canterburyhs.ocdsb.ca

Claude Watson Arts Program (public)
100 Princess Avenue
North York, Ontario M2N 0A8
416-395-3210
Disciplines: ballet, modern dance, composition
http://claudewatson.ca/site/

Ecole Secondaire publique De La Salle (public)
501, Ancienne rue St-Patrick
Ottawa, Ontario K1N 8R3
613-789-0053
Disciplines: ballet, modern dance
www.de-la-salle.cepeo.on.ca

Etobicoke School for the Arts (public)
675 Royal York Road
Toronto, Ontario M8Y 2T1
416-394-6910
Disciplines: ballet, modern dance, jazz
www.esainfo.ca

Langley Fine Arts School (public)
9096 Trattle Street
Fort Langley, British Columbia V1M 2S6
604-888-3113
Disciplines: modern dance, choreography, history, yoga, Pilates,
    cultural
http://langleyfinearts.com/contact.htm

Mayfield Secondary School (public)
5000 Mayfield Road
Caledon, Ontario L7C 0Z5
905-846-6060
Disciplines: ballet, modern dance, dance history, cultural,
    choreography
http://schools.peelschools.org/sec/mayfield/Pages/default.aspx

Sudbury Secondary School (magnet)
154 College Street
Sudbury, Ontario P3C 4Y2
705-674-7551
Disciplines: ballet, modern dance, jazz, world dance
http://sudburysecondary.net

Unionville High School, Arts Program (public)
201 Town Centre Boulevard
Unionville, Ontario L3Y 4V8
416-479-2787
Disciplines: ballet, modern dance, jazz, multicultural dance, musi-
    cal theatre, performance
www.artsunionville.com

Victoria School of the Arts (public)
10210-108 Avenue
Edmonton, Alberta T5H 1A8
780-426-3010

Disciplines: ballet, modern dance, jazz
http://victoria-school.ca

In Australia

Campbelltown Performing Arts High School (private)
P.O. Box 561
Campbelltown, New South Wales 2560
02-4625-1403
Disciplines: general dance focus
http://pc.cpahs.nsw.edu.au

Golden Grove High School (public)
1 Adey Place
Golden Grove, South Australia 5125
08-8282-6400
Disciplines: ballet, modern dance, composition, conditioning, jazz, tap, musical theatre, dance theory, dance history, anatomy, nutrition
www.goldengrovehs.sa.edu.au/

Newtown High School of the Performing Arts (public)
P.O. Box 785
Newtown, New South Wales 2042
612-9519-1657
Disciplines: ballet, modern dance, production
http://web1.newtown-h.schools.nsw.edu.au

Victorian College of the Arts Secondary School (public)
57 Miles Street
Southbank, Victoria 3006
03-8644-8644
Disciplines: ballet, contemporary, jazz, world dance
www.vcass.vic.edu.au/

Wollongong High School of the Performing Arts (public)
Lysaght Street
Fairy Meadow New South Wales 2519
02-4229-6844
Disciplines: ballet, contemporary, tap, musical theatre
www.wollongong-h.schools.nsw.edu.au/curriculum-activities/dance

Students from the School of Madison Ballet, Madison, Wisconsin. ©2015
Maureen Janson

GLOSSARY

adagio Slow, fluid, and graceful motions practiced in a ballet class.

Alexander technique A somatic method in which the body is educated with a goal of eliminating unnecessary tension by reducing bad habits and encouraging proper alignment. First developed by Frederick Matthias Alexander (1869–1955).

anorexia Also known as anorexia nervosa, an eating disorder in which one drops to extremely low body weight. The disorder is generally coupled with emotional stress, a fear of gaining weight, and a distorted perception of body image.

barre The wood or metal handrail used by dancers during the warm-up part of a ballet class. Barre, or barre work, also refers to the entire warm-up portion of the class, which is followed by centre work (performed away from the barre in the center of the studio).

Cecchetti method A style of ballet developed by Enrico Cecchetti (1850–1928). This structured and graded style aims at simplicity of line in the body, and trains the dancer to work independently of the teacher.

character dance Part of the classical ballet repertoire, character is a dance style representing European folk dances or other national dances.

Dance Magazine The most influential monthly American dance publication first introduced in 1927 and still published today.

deportment Manners and behavior.

entrechat The French term for a ballet jump in which the dancer executes a quick cross of the legs and feet, resulting in a sharp beating motion.

Feldenkrais A somatic practice developed by Moshe Feldenkrais (1904–1984) initially as a method of pain reduction. Through body awareness exercises, the method also focuses on an increase in flexibility and a sense of general well-being.

kinesiology The study of human movement.

Louis XIV (1638–1715) King of France from 1643–1715, lover of ballet and gifted, majestic, and virtuosic performer. Danced in roughly 40 ballets in a diverse range of solo roles.

Marley A type of durable vinyl commonly used for dance studio and stage flooring.

metatarsals Tube-shaped bones in the middle of the foot, connecting toes to the ankle.

moleskin A type of cotton fabric. Refers to adhesive pads made of moleskin commonly used by dancers to prevent blisters on the feet.

musculature The particular arrangement of a muscle or group of muscles within the human muscular system.

neophyte A beginner; one who is new to ballet studies.

neuromuscular connections The synaptic junction between nerve with muscle fibers (cells), eventually resulting in the contraction of a muscle.

petit rat French term referring to a young dancer who trains at the Paris Opera ballet school and who might appear on stage in opera performances.

Pilates Joseph Pilates (1883–1967) developed this physical fitness method for increasing flexibility, strength, control, and endurance through a series of alignment and breathing exercises. Pilates is heavily practiced by dancers as a method of cross-training.

pirouette A ballet turning motion executed on one foot.

pointe An advanced aspect of ballet; dancing by supporting body weight on the tips of the toes. Pointe work requires special shoes (pointe shoes), and proper alignment, developed musculature, and appropriate technique and training.

pronation A rolling inward of the foot, with weight predominantly toward the big toe. A common occurrence in those who are flat-footed.

repertory Choreographed ballets that are maintained and performed repeatedly over time by a particular dance company or companies.

rosin A type of pine (or other conifer) resin used by dancers on the tips of pointe shoes to reduce slippage.

Royal Academy of Dance Founded in London in 1920 to improve the standard of teaching ballet. This organization offers teacher training programs and certifications.

solfège A method commonly used to teach pitch and sight-reading in music.

somatics Movement studies that emphasize internal physical perception rather than how the body is perceived externally, as in a performance. Somatic methods include Alexander technique, Feldenkrais, and Pilates.

synaptic connections Within the nervous system, the passing of electrical or chemical signals to any other cells in the body, assisting in the storage of information and memory.

turnout Outward rotation of the hip, and in turn, the rest of the leg, allowing for greater speed and range of motion in the leg within ballet training.

Vaganova method Russian style of ballet technique devised by Agrippina Vaganova (1879–1951). Fusing French and Italian styles this method aims to train the full body in harmony.

Students from the School of Madison Ballet, Madison, Wisconsin. ©2015
Maureen Janson

SUGGESTED FURTHER READING

Anderson, Jack. *Ballet and Modern Dance: A Concise History.* Princeton, NJ: Princeton Book Company, 1993. A very useful and entertaining book offering an overview of dance history. Short profiles at the end of the book provide a "Who's Who" of dance-world personalities.

Barringer, Janice, and Sarah Schlesinger. *The Pointe Book: Shoes, Training and Technique.* Princeton, NJ: Princeton Book Company, 2012, 3rd ed. The most complete treatise on what it takes to dance on your toes. Includes a history of the dancer's rise onto pointe.

Beaumont, Cyril. *Michel Fokine and His Ballets.* Brooklyn, NY: Dance Horizons, 1981.

Berardi, Gigi. *Finding Balance: Fitness, Training, and Health for a Lifetime in Dance* New York: Routledge, 2005. Provide details on injury prevention and longevity of career and life in dance.

Blasis, Carlo. *The Code of Terpsichore, a Treatise on the Art of Dancing.* London, E. Bull, 1830. Documentation of the earliest ballet technique, theory, and history.

Brown, Jean Morrison, ed. *The Vision of Modern Dance.* Princeton, NJ: Princeton Book Company, 1998, 2nd ed. Essays by the pioneers of modern dance.

Buckle, Richard. *In Search of Diaghilev*. London: Sidgwick Publishers, 1955. Buckle is the foremost expert on Diaghilev.

Cohen, Selma Jean, ed. *Dance As a Theatre Art: Source Readings in Dance History from 1581 to the Present*. 2nd ed. Princeton, NJ: Princeton Book Company, 1991.

Demidov, Alexandre. *Russian Ballet Past and Present*. New York: Doubleday, 1977.

Duncan, Isadora. *My Life*. New York: Liveright, 1927. For a less subjective account of Duncan's life, see Victor Seroff's *The Real Isadora*. New York: Dial, 1971.

Ellfeldt, Lois. *From Magic to Art*, Dubuque, IA: Wm. C. Brown, 1976. A comprehensive look at dance through the ages. Includes enlightening quotes from critics, teachers, dancers, and choreographers.

Feldenkrais, Moshe. *Awareness through Movement*. New York: HarperCollins, 1990.

Fleming, Gladys Andrews, ed. *Children's Dance*. Washington, DC: American Alliance for Health, Physical Education, Recreation, and Dance Press, 1973. Recommended dance activities for children from the ages of three to twelve.

Franklin, Eric. *Conditioning for Dance, Training for peak performance in all dance forms*. Champaign, IL: Human Kinetics, 2004. Advice and exercises for increasing strength, balance and flexibility in order to improve dance skills.

Friedman, Philip, and Gail Eisen. *The Pilates Method of Mental and Physical Conditioning*. New York: Penguin, 2005.

Gordon, Suzanne. *Off Balance: The Real World of Ballet*. New York: Pantheon, 1983. A brutally honest account of the dancing life in New York.

Graham, Martha. *Blood Memory*. New York: Doubleday, 1991. Graham's autobiography.

Hammond, Sandra Noll. *Ballet Basics* (2004) 5th ed. New York: McGraw-Hill; *Beyond the Basics* (2010). Long Grove, IL: Waveland Press, Inc. Both books provide easy-to-read guidelines to technique as well as general information about the dance world.

Humphrey, Doris. *The Art of Making Dances*. Princeton, NJ: Princeton Book Company, 1990. Practical guide and handbook for would-be choreographers.

Kirkland, Gelsey, and Greg Lawrence. *Dancing On My Grave.* New York: Doubleday, 1986. A heartrending account of the life of one of America's greatest ballerinas.

Kirstein, Lincoln. *Portrait of Mr. B.* New York: Viking, 1984. A biographical essay on George Balanchine, with numerous photos.

Latimer, Jane Evans. *Living Binge Free.* Boulder, CO: Livingquest, 1988. A guide to conquering compulsive eating.

Laws, Kenneth. *The Physics of Dance.* New York: Schirmer Books, 1984. Dance movement explained scientifically.

Mara, Thalia. *First Steps in Ballet; Second Steps in Ballet; Third Steps in Ballet; On Your Toes.* Princeton, NJ: Princeton Book Company, 1987. Perfect reading for young dancers.

Martin, John. *The Modern Dance.* Brooklyn, NY: Dance Horizons 1965. A series of lectures, originally given in 1931 and 1932, outlining the philosophy of early modern dance pioneers.

Paskevska, Anna. *Both Sides of the Mirror: The Science and Art of Ballet.* Brooklyn, NY: Dance Horizons, 1981. 2nd ed. by Princeton Book Company, 1992.

Paskevska, Anna. *Ballet. From the First Plié to Mastery.* New York: Routledge, 2002.

Paskevska, Anna. *Ballet Beyond Tradition.* New York, NY: Routledge, 2005.

Rone, Elvira and Fernau Hall. *Olga Preobrazhenskaya: a Portrait.* New York: Marcel Dekker, 1978. A loving biography of the great ballerina.

Scholl, Tim. *From Petipa to Balanchine, Classical Revival and the Modernisation of Ballet.* New York: Routledge, 2004. Contemporary look at the evolution and history of Russian Ballet.

Shook, Karel. *Elements of Classical Ballet Technique.* Brooklyn, NY: Dance Horizons, 1977. A treatise on the classical technique as practiced at the Dance Theatre of Harlem in New York.

Simmel, Liane. *Dance Medicine in Practice-Anatomy, Injury Prevention, Training.* New York: Routledge, 2014.

Solomon, Ruth, Sandra C. Minton, and John Solomon, eds. *Preventing Dance Injuries*, 2nd ed. Champaign, IL: Human Kinetics, 2005.

Sorell, Walter. *The Dance Through the Ages.* Putnam Publishing Group, 1967.

Spignesi, Angelyn. *Starving Women*. Dallas, TX: Spring Publications, 1983.

Steinberg, Laurence D., with Benson Brown and Sanford Dornbusch. *Beyond the Classroom*. Simon & Schuster, 1996.

Stransky, Judith, and Robert B. Stone. *The Alexander Technique: Joy in the Life of Your Body*. New York: Beaufort Books, 1981.

Vaganova, Agrippina. *Basic Principles of Classical Ballet: Russian Ballet Technique*. New York: Dover Publications, 1946.

Vincent, L. M., MD. *Competing with the Sylph: Dancers and the Pursuit of the Ideal Body Form*. 2nd ed. Princeton, NJ: Princeton Book Company, 1980. Should be required reading for every aspiring dancer.

Watkins, Andrea and Priscilla M. Clarkson, *Dancing Longer Dancing Stronger*, Princeton, NJ: Princeton Book Company, 1994.

Wigman, Mary. *The Language of Dance*. Trans, by Walter Sorrell. Middletown, CT: Wesleyan University Press, 1966. Descriptions of the dances that Wigman composed.

Wright, Stuart. *Dancer's Guide to Injuries of the Lower Extremities*. Cranbury, NJ: Cornwall Books, 1985.

INDEX